Of the Imagination

You! Are the Creator

TERMINA ASHTON

Copyright © 2014 by Termina Ashton
All rights reserved. No part of this book may be reproduced,
scanned, or distributed in any printed or electronic form without
permission.
First Edition: April 2014
ISBN- 13: 978-0-9954076-0-2
ISBN-10: 0995407606

To All That Was, Is And Will Be Around Me,
Your Existence Gives Me Inspiration.

This book is designed to provide information and inspiration to readers. It is sold with the understanding that the author is not engaged to render any type of psychological, legal, or any other kind of professional advice. The content of each article is the sole expression and opinion of its author. No warranties or guarantees are expressed or implied by the author's choice to include any of the content in this volume. The author shall have no liability or responsibility to any person or entity regarding physical, psychological, emotional, financial, commercial damages, special, incidental, or consequential by the information contained in this book.

CONTENTS

Foreword	3
Introduction	5
Preface	9

Part I: To Expound or To Impound

Define or Confine	17
Imagination IS everything	28
Shroud of unknowing	34
I, Imagine	41
Unshackle the giant within	48

Part II: Who was I?

Conditioned tempering	60
Impress or Distress	69
The evasive clone carousel	76
Subservient to whom?	94
I am my own creation	103
Choice of illusion	109

Part III: You! Are the Creator

Three wishes granted	128
Cause of life	144

Beacon body	152
I give to you a magic pen	170
Misplaced memory	185

Part IV: Festival Blueprint

Imagination feeds imagination	191
The unilateral covenant	196
'Top Secret' Unmasked	204
Lost! But now I'm found	213
What if?	230
Action the brew in my head	236
Collection and scraps	239
Sift and flow	241
Developing a birth	243
What's your fancy?	246
Design and plot	249

Conclusion and your awaiting future	259
Acknowledgement	271
About the Author	273

Foreword

For years I have been blessed to work with many authors from all over the world. Termina is one of those extraordinary authors who I have been blessed to serve. My own reputation has been built by delivering valuable services and offering sound advice that can, when followed, result in phenomenal success. Termina is one of those extraordinary people who truly follow through.

One of the best things an author can do for their career is to share their own unique story. And, if self-help is the genre they choose to be in, share their story in a way that offers effective guidance to their readers. This is precisely what Termina has done so magnificently with this book.

Termina has a lot of experience, insights and wisdom to offer. She shares the concept of using one of our greatest faculties that can contribute to positive change; the use of our imagination.

As you read this brilliant book allow yourself to be open to the ideas. Allow your imagination to open up (like an umbrella it works better when it is open).

It doesn't take a lot of words or hundreds and hundreds of pages of content to have you experience a radical shift in your thinking. There are many times throughout this book where you'll find inspiration in only a few words. As an example, Termina writes: *"when a thought is triggered and through the incredible power of a decision, followed by action, even the smallest step will lead the way in achieving the result, our goal"* and she is absolutely right! I have experienced this myself on many occasions and observed others doing the same.

Allow Termina's story to be the nudge to have you conjure up your goal and see it materialize in your life. You have the power within you to create anything you desire. Go ahead and put these wise ideas into practice and watch your life change in the most glorious ways.

Peggy McColl

New York Times Best-Selling Author

Introduction

One of the high moments that has enriched my life came the day I found out who I was.

This unforgettable experience produced an identification; an absolute recognition that contrasted what I believed my life to be. When I finished the meditation I came back to present reality with a start.

Herein is a message for the unidentified person who is holding this book. It contains essentials for thoughts and teachings of our imagination also revealing the impact upon mind, and how it profoundly affects us. Included throughout this book is a system to aid in illuminating and activating what is known as high frequencies or raised frequencies so that the reader may unlock and begin to radiate their own unique energy signature.

Have you ever thought about why you have certain experiences? What your driving stimulus is? What keeps you desiring more or even less? How to gain good health, fulfilling relationships, happiness and comfortable finances in one great package? And what is responsible for the hardships you have endured?

Just as many others I simply wanted to be happy, have no concerns, remove the carried burdens, move forward, and find that purpose that makes me want to wake up each morning in cheer, breathe in life and feel the gratitude for my blessings.

This craving led me to search, seek answers, and ask for help from all who shared information on success principles. The paths many times became overwhelming, confusing, exhausting, frustrating or empty; with unfulfilled hopes bringing no results, wasted time, lack of evidence and a decreasing bank account. I accumulated a clutter of books, audios and videos proclaiming promises of a greater life, which only brought greater debt for the purchase and more worry of how I was ever going to get ahead, and the ever growing expenses of the advancing world only increased my concerns.

Through the teachings of these success principles I was aware of one aspect, be positive! Because like attracts like, and thoughts become things. I just needed to keep my chin up and keep moving forward. I actioned this often, even though I didn't understand what keep moving forward really meant. I wrote in my journal, I did the tasks set by the teachers of the books, audios or self-help programs, only to find again and again I was chasing another pipe dream, and disappointment the only real evidence. This added more resistance to my beliefs and blurred my beliefs of allowing possibilities. I was frustrated; it's all just crap! I am being positive and I try to see the good in everything. Some people are just not meant to have success, you can't have it all, life wasn't meant to be easy, we all can't have good health, fulfilling relationships, happiness and comfortable finances in one great package, right!

Then the answer came!

And this same identification can be yours.

I wish to share my experience by helping others reawaken the festival of their imagination. Within everyone there contains a giant of possibilities. Everyone CAN see their ideas and desires come into fruition. And everyone CAN unlock their own unique energy signature.

This book serves to be a helpful source of guidance, please respect the special nature of its contents. As you read through, you will find that a question you had on an earlier page will find an answer on a later page. You will also find the power within words and why it is an all important part of the recipe for personal successful outcomes. Festival of the Imagination contains sections arranged in progressive order. By the time you read and ponder all of them, it will help you determine if you are being directed toward your true power, your giant within, your unconditional, infinite and absolute thoughts.

Preface

IMAGINE... A life you truly want and it comes to you with ease.

IMAGINE... You live without fear, doubt or limits.

IMAGINE... That you have just uncovered a mystery and the secrets contained within give you clarity and you say goodbye to confusion, frustration or hardship.

If we were to ask someone who does not have a hefty bank balance to purchase something such as a yacht, and to do this by imagining the sale, they would usually do this without resistance (make a stand against, oppose). When one 'imagines' they do not see this as a real event. It's just play acting or a mind-game. Much like a fantasy. However, if we were to ask this same someone to purchase this yacht in reality, the critical mind will automatically object, and recoil with responses such as; how? Are you crazy? It costs too much, I don't want one anyway, or I don't like yachts. They would see this as a ridiculous request and the natural reaction is to expel a list of the impossibilities involved.

What if this person was to win the yacht, would they gladly take it, regardless of whether they like it or not? After all they could sell it, right!

When we imagine we stimulate the unconscious mind, the deeper mind, and bypass the critical mind, also known as the conscious mind and what's more ingenious is the brain does not separate what is fact from fiction. It accepts an imagined thought and a thought derived from reality to be of equal value. At no point does the brain think a picture of a car, even if it is only an imagined thought, to be any different to you actually looking at or touching a real one. This also applies to emotions. If we are watching a dramatic movie and our emotions are heightened - feeling the characters' pain, joy or fear, our brain will recognise this as truth playing out in our real life experience.

What does this mean to us? A great deal in fact. It is our life! When we understand the disguises, beacons and the power of introspection we place ourselves in a position to reset our outcomes and bring into our experiences whatever we desire.

Why it is that many say children have a great imagination? Why should the realm of imagination be solely the domain of children? We may grow to become adults but we are still that same person we were back in our youth, our brain is still enveloped within, it is not as though someone came along and removed it and replaced it with another. Nor did we receive a vaccination to prevent the risk of childhood thought infecting our adult mind.

When we were younger we found joy and comfort in our imagination. We lived our days through make-believe, characters and experiences that occupied our thoughts in many ways and did not feel this to be inappropriate behaviour, that is not until we were told to 'stop daydreaming', followed by reasons as to why this was not good behaviour, such as; you're not listening. We then listened to whatever reasoning was given, obeyed, and focused our concentration to the said task. And by listening to repeated reasons of what bad behaviour was, as adults we have managed to successfully suppress our friendship with the unconditional imagination. We placed a 'no go zone" reason to avoid experiencing what we so loved to do during our childhood and it is this rejection of fantasy play that now governs our behaviour at an automatic subconscious level.

True growing up is to grow from within. To accept and know that, regardless of the passing years, our inner core never changes, only the outside influences cloud us. We carry with us a sync sabotage influenced by a nocebo effect.

New seeded thoughts overlap our unconditional thoughts, our unlimited, infinite and absolute thoughts, unrestricted by conditions, just as we had from childhood and regrettably this purity in thinking develops into a sleeping giant or so we believe. The sleeping giant is our greatest faculty, boundless imagination, and more importantly imagination IS a crucial ingredient to living the life we truly want when we know how it is used.

As do many children I too as a child had a vivid imagination, a mind brimming with unconditioned thoughts, then life crept through and my thoughts were progressively conditioned, I was taught the lesson of growing up and becoming responsible.

It was 1995, I became a single parent with a toddler, my finances were scarce, I had an empty bank account, seventy-five cents in my purse, no home and a trailer load consisting mainly of toddler items. The bones on the left side of my body were broken, which I put much effort in hiding the pain (as no one would want to employ me if they knew the extent of my injuries). It's quite powerful what a person will overcome and accomplish when their 'why' is so strong. I managed to gain employment at three places, one was stacking shelves at a supermarket in the evenings and all this for my why; to build on everyday living essentials such as food, electricity and furnishings for our humble rental home.

So there I was, a single mum, worn out by my work schedule, my recovering body and the demands of an active toddler yet to my surprise it was at this adverse time in my life I discovered an unexpected freedom. I had no time for sorrow, or for the fears that crept through daily, my daily routines prevented it, and without influences in our home I was able to make my own decisions as well as observe the joy my daughter brought to my daily life.

My busy days and my new founded liberty had started a momentum in breaking the surface of my habitual ways, however, I remained clueless. I was changing within yet did not realise at that time the importance of my transitional path. I believed, as I was the only adult household member, I must be responsible and was compelled to do things because as an adult we must be the providers, the carers, build on our needs and get our heads out of the clouds. It was in this year that the same compelling force triggered an urge, the urge to bring to fruition an idea. I decided to create and build my first piece of woodwork - a rocking horse. And it was not until years later that I realized this was the glorious trigger to my transition, the stimulant to unconditional revival and the powerful process in altering my DNA.

Our present experiences are a result of our yesterday, and our future will be a response from today. We make choices each and every day about our life, even though we believe them to be thoughts rather than choices. It is the beliefs regarding these choices that gives to us our daily experiences, whether they be enjoyable or despised.

There is an easy formula in attaining your goals or desires in any or all areas of life you choose. Do you want success, good health, great relationships, laughter, love or simply a better tomorrow? Like magic, we CAN create the experiences we want, and it begins with re-discovering something that has been disguised by patterns and by understanding the power of the imagination.

You do not have to wait for this to unfold. Our mind is the data bank of ALL human consciousness and the vault is stored with every memory including; our unconditional, limitless thoughts, all our hopes, all our desires, inventions that were dreamed, beliefs we previously had, and this gives us our true personalities, our true identity when we choose to unlock it.

I rediscovered there was more *to* me; I sensed there

was more *in* me. And this is true of ALL people, they are more than they presently know. Not only did I ask myself this question: How did I get to where I am? I felt I was meant to be more than what I had become and did not have to just tolerate my standard existence. I wanted to experience more than I had, and it was this piercing feeling, this urge from my intimate friend - discontentment, that grew to become a flame of possibilities; and this activated the formula to finding ones' true happiness and purpose.

I find it refreshing and am grateful for the day I *revived*.

I am awake, I am now master of my life and I create all that I desire, you can too! Allow me to be your reminder. You really can have, be, do what you choose, it exists and is awaiting your return.

'Imagination is everything. It is the preview of life's coming attractions'. *Albert Einstein*

Part I

TO EXPOUND OR

TO IMPOUND

Define or Confine

Here we begin with a fundamental principle. An all-important matter: awareness. There are essential ingredients that must be understood as a basis for successfully creating chosen outcomes. It is the foundation of awareness that will determine how the result appears, how strongly, and how long outcomes are to last, therefore it is imperative in understanding how to activate and start a solid foundation to attain desired outcomes. This following chapter is a fundamental foundation and others will be unmasked in the following chapters.

What is Imagination?

It depends on who is answering it!

The Oxford dictionary states:

- The faculty or action of forming new ideas; images or concepts of external objects not present to the senses.
- The part of the mind that imagines things.

The Merriam-Webster dictionary states:

- The ability to imagine things that are not real.
- The ability to form a picture in your mind of something that you have not seen or experienced.

The urban dictionary states:

- Creations of the mind triggered by a thought.
- A virtual space of creativity inside your brain.
- That magical point in your life when you think your crush likes you back... (...Um?)

With so many definitions. It's a no wonder why some are confused and some from other countries find the English language to be one of the hardest languages to learn. We add to or change definitions as we go, we change the spelling or abbreviate a word, we create slang words; we also have heteronym words. A word that has the same spelling as another word but has a different sound and a different meaning. For example;

Tear - *(tare)* tear that paper; *(teer)* I can see a tear rolling down the cheek.

Wound – *(woond)* a gashing wound on the leg from the fall; *(wownd)* I'm wound up.

Bow - *(rhymes with how)* bow to the King; *(rhymes with "tow")* bow and arrow.

Dove - *(rhymes with "love")* a bird; *(rhymes with stove)* He dove into the water.

Now... Let's look at another definition of the imagination, this time from the Etymology dictionary. Etymology is the study of the history of words, their origins, and how their form and meaning have changed over time.

From Latin *imaginationem* "imagination, a fancy".

What about the word Fancy?

Mid-15c., *fantsy* "inclination, liking."

Why is this important to know?

Albert Einstein told us this; *"Everything is energy and that's all there is to it. Match the frequency of the reality you want and you cannot help but get that reality. It can be no other way. This is not philosophy. This is physics."*

"Everything is Energy." This has been proven many times by Nobel Prize winning physicists, such as Niels Bohr, including numerous scientists and quantum physicists from past to present. Things we can see, including us, and that which cannot been seen is energy. And all energy has

conscious intent. A purpose, goal and end result.

Thoughts, words, and emotions are also energy; and when created carry with it conscious intent to bring into our physical experience the exact match of the frequency we relay.

When a word is first created it first appears as thought in the imagination. The inventor of any particular word, imagined this word and in that same moment they also had a particular sensation, or, as we call it, emotion; just as we all have emotions in every moment. We are never without emotional sensation, we could be happy, sad, calm, frustrated, serene or angry, and this can change from moment to moment.

When a word is invented the alphabetic combination creates a sound. This sound and the emotion felt by the inventor in that moment merge and create a pattern, a pattern of a unique frequency and this originates into another 'something' that has conscious intent.

The conscious intent or unique frequency (purpose, goal and end result) of any word can be distorted, veiled or muffled when used in the wrong context with the unique frequency of another word/s. Therefore it is essential for us to be mindful of context, correct word and sound as an important part of our language when we are to choose exactly what we want.

All words have origins. Many English words have been borrowed from others known as root or origin words, for example; Anglo-Saxon, German, Greek, Latin, or French. And the root words are the ones that hold power (unique frequency), immense power, when they were created.

The words we speak or write come from our thoughts. Whether the words are spoken, thought or written they impact our outcomes in life, and regardless of what new or expanded definition is attached to them, the only frequency that counts is the sound and the original meaning of the word. When we don't use a word in context to the original meaning we confine our possibilities and this can block our path to abundance.

When a word is used in its correct context with its original meaning this is known as illuminating and activating. Throughout this book I have included phrases and powerful words to assist in illuminating and activating your path to abundance. This is a critical key when speaking, thinking or writing words, particularly for desired outcomes in your life experiences.

Many words have had contrasting and altered definitions applied throughout the years. We use many words and often we are unaware to the true and initial definition. We only know the definition that was passed onto us, and what we read in the remodeled dictionaries.

Here are a few examples of original words and the altered definitions;

Fun: from verb *fun* (1680s) "to cheat, hoax." Altered: "Something that provides mirth or amusement: enjoyment or playfulness."

Manifest: from Latin *manifestare*, "to discover, disclose, betray." Altered: "Readily perceived by the eye or the understanding; evident; obvious; apparent. Plain."

Demon: from Latin *daemon* "spirit," from PIE **daimon-* "divider, provider." Altered: "An evil spirit; devil or fiend."

Gin: from c. 1200, *ginnen*, "to begin." Altered: "An alcoholic liquor obtained by distilling grain mash with juniper berries." Also in Australia, this is an offensive slang word directed towards an indigenous woman.

Heretic: from Greek *hairetikos* "able to choose." Altered: Religion was attached to it. A baptized Roman

Catholic who willfully and persistently rejects any article of faith."

Awesome : from *awe* (n.) + *-some* .

'Awe': from c.1300, *aue*, "fear, terror, great reverence," earlier *aghe*, c. 1200, from a Scandinavian source, Old Norse *agi* "fright;"

'–Some': from Old English *–sum*, "tending to; causing; to a considerable degree."

"Fear causing or terror causing." Altered: Slang "very impressive."

Lady: from Old English *hlæfdige* "one who kneads bread." Altered: "A woman who is refined, polite, and well-spoken." Hmm. I think I'll pass on being called a lady. I don't particularly see myself as a bread kneader.

Not so long ago the largest English dictionary contained 2.9 million entries, and this continues to increase. More than half of these entries have altered meanings for words. This increase in word form and added definitions can disempower our ability to create what we desire. Each letter within a word carries meaning and has its own vibration (unique frequency). It is the combined total of these letters and emotion when invented that creates the frequency of the result, and the original definition is what we are creating.

I was surprised when I began to explore the origins and meanings of words that I used often. I explored this further with a friend who is a wordsmith, one who is an expert with words. We both were astounded to find a significant amount of words we assumed to know the definitions to, and discovered we were clouded by the influences of cultural conditionings, the beliefs and interpretations shared to us from our families, schools and the environment surrounding us from past to present. And it is this absence of awareness that can create our unwanted experiences.

Every sound we convey and every word we think sends out a frequency, an energy stream that creates our reality. We attract like energy, like attracts like, the Law of Attraction. And because of tampered definitions and lack in awareness, we are either improving or destroying our health, relationships, or our prosperity automatically. The Law of Attraction is listening to our transmissions, disregarding whether we know or do not know what the frequency means, and giving us what we ask for, every time.

Success in all areas of life comes in part from communication with our thoughts, to ourselves, to and from others. We use words to relay these thoughts, concepts, ideas, images and intentions. It is essential that we develop an awareness of our thought process as well as the way we and others around us use language by practising words as they were designed to be used and understand what particular outcomes they carry. We can choose to Define with the truest definition or stay on automatic and Confine our ability to create abundance.

Words are a command to our thoughts and this IS a way we create energy (frequency). When we speak, we also think, which doubles the transmission with the Law of Attraction. To forward our opportunity towards abundance we can choose to quit (release, let go, relinquish) using the words that hold us back and replace them with power words that will serve us well. Words that will increase and align our energetic experience. Because, everything is energy. Including words!

Our practised interpretations passed onto us from our environment are either helping, hampering or even blocking our easy path to abundance and we do this unconsciously. Take back the control of the energies you emit. Start by writing a list of the common phrases and words you use then research the origin. Understand these words you use including those voiced by others. Gain comprehension of the true meaning as well as pronunciation in order to unleash the power of words you choose, and this will cooperate in creating what you desire rather than a blockage of your abundance. When you come across a powerful word, use it repeatedly. I often say 'wonderful' and find no need to speak any other word to describe: *full of or having marvelous things and miracles.* And when I speak or journal, I use the word as wunderfoll. As it was originally intended.

You do not need a large vocabulary to create your desired life. There are successful people who are illiterate, and those who have wealth, health and happiness with very small vocabularies. Heed the advice from some wise masters throughout the centuries, "use less words" or "less is more."

When you next make a wish, a choice or say an affirmation, check what you are actually transmitting. As the old adage goes, "be careful what you wish for."

As stated earlier, throughout this book are phrases and powerful words to assist in illuminating and activating your path to abundance. You will also notice some repetition. This has been done intentionally to also assist with illuminating and activating. Here are some powerful words to get you started:

Power words:

Accept (*accepter*), faith (*faith, feith, fei, fai*), love (*lufu*), hilarious (*hilaris*), joy (*joie*), supreme (*superus*), bliss (*blis*), bless (*bletsian*), tranquillity (*tranquilite*), absolute (*absolut*), achieve (*achever*), worthy (*axios*), *magic (magique)*, happy/wealth (*ead*), abundance *(abundare),* feel *(felan),* good *(god- say with long 'o),* perfect *(parfiten, creative (creatus).*

Power phrases:

For my gain.

Super serene.

Bright eyes.

Guidance from the angels.

"Words are free. It's how you use them that may cost you." –*Kushand*

"Handle them carefully, for words have more power than atom bombs."- *Ira Gassen*

"The pen is mightier than the sword." - *Edward Bulwer-Lytton*

Imagination <u>IS</u> everything

The word imagination in past years and today carries many definitions. Good and bad. It all depends on what we were taught such as; what is appropriate behaviour and what is required of a male, a female, an age group or what is considered to be time wasting and not paying attention.

Everything begins in the imagination!

If everything began in the imagination where did opinions come from?

They all began in someone's imagination. Nothing can exist without it first appearing in the imagination. Every idea, every belief, every tangible thing and every opinion.

So... Why is there still a negative view on the use of the imagination? Especially when it only means "A fancy." Some perceive it as child's play, or something artists and musicians have because of their eccentric ways or drug habits. Some scold others, in particular children, when they are 'off with the fairies" or 'daydreaming again".

- Get your head out of the clouds
- Grow up
- Act your age; or,
- where on earth do you get your ideas from?

Any of this sound familiar? It does for me. I heard some of these, even as I grew to become an adult.

Misconceptions regarding the work of the imagination are common and as I discovered when conducting interviews there are many views, both positive and negative on this subject. Therefore, let me describe what I have learned about this plain and simple word, and practice.

Many think the imagination is something to be achieved, something only some are good at, a fantasy or to fantasise something extravagant, farfetched or whimsical. Something fantastic that is strange, weird or not of this world. Something distorted, absurd or preposterous. And as stated earlier childs' play.

<u>Imagination IS</u> the use of our mind and mental creative ability. It is what we do every day, every moment and what we have done to achieve the results we have

experienced. Remember...Nothing can exist without it first appearing in the imagination! Imagination is the mind. And our mind never sleeps.

When we accept a definition of any opinion, this becomes belief and results as attachment. We place ourselves in a prison of opinions and are unaware of our incarceration. Attachment to a belief will confine our mindset and add limitations to our experiences in life; and attachments will create our outcomes.

Everything we see, everything we know, every word we use and every definition attached to our beliefs, ALL began as fantasy, concepts unrestricted by reality. A fantasy within the mind, the imagination. There is nothing, NOTHING! created from past to present that did not originate first from the imagination. We, humanity, created and create as we go, in an ever expanding world of need and desire. *Necessity is the mother of all invention.* – Plato

All that we know, see, hear, taste and feel becomes our experience when we attach belief to it. We, just as our parents, ancestors and societies, exist, act and think with fantasies created by others, others from history.

Our mind, our imagination is our "heart". It is the force and the essence that brings to us our reality. We are using our imagination at all times, even when we accept a belief we are using our imagination.

In both the Old and New Testament of the bible the word "heart" is used. This does not refer to a vital organ; a muscle that pumps blood through the body, or; romance, feelings or literary definitions. It refers to the whole innermost part of the human, our MINDS; our essence, our totality.

It is through our totality we accept or reject that which can become our physical experience. When we understand what imagination is we can learn to become masters of our experiences. Life is not happening to us, it is happening for us and it is how we choose to use our imagination that will produce the harvest or hardship of our physical existence.

"Watch over your heart with all diligence, for from it flow the springs of life." - Proverbs 4:23

Clarity of thought, be it fiction, or non-fiction, develops from the imagination. Life experience develops from the imagination. Every conditioned belief is developed first from the imagination. And imagination is thought in production. Production and replication for the Law of Attraction. Any thought held in the imagination becomes an idea, and an idea has definite potential of being life's coming attraction, a belief, your story or your physical life experience! Exactly as Einstein stated; *'Imagination is everything. It is the preview of life's coming attractions'.*

Pay attention to how you spend your time. Are your thoughts joyful, or full of words of frustration, lack or impossibilities? You have nothing more precious than time. In any one moment of time, abundance may be gained or lost. We are given time in sequence, one instant after another and never simultaneously. We only need to experience the present moment.

"I never think of the future. It comes soon enough." –
Albert Einstein

And in the present moment, we can do whatever it takes to make us feel good, we can evolve to whatever we choose. We can Imagine... We carry this power of choice and imagination with us always.

"Imagination is more important than knowledge. The true sign of intelligence is not knowledge but imagination." -
Albert Einstein

Imagination is...

From Latin *imaginationem* "imagination, a fancy".

Fancy…

From mid-15c., *fantsy* "inclination, liking." A contraction of fantasy. "Inclination, whim, desire." Meaning "the productive imagination"

Fantasy…

From *phantazein*, "to make visible, display."

Festival…

From *festival,* "suitable for a feast; solemn, magnificent, joyful, happy. Time set aside"

Festival of the Imagination:

"Time set aside to make visible."

Shroud of unknowing

Awareness of who you are is your first step to stop from sinking deeper into the illusionary world of lack and limitation. We live in "darkness". Not the darkness of an evening when the moon is out, or, the darkness of not knowing who we truly are; anyone can imagine this darkness. Darkness results from a lack of knowledge, and knowledge is "acknowledgment of a superior". The darkness we live in is the lack to admit, speak up and to BE who we truly are. And it is the unspoken words that places us into the cloud of unknowing.

Consciousness:

From *conscius*,"knowing, aware." Emerges from a sole action.

Acknowledgement!

From *aknow*, "understand, recognize, Admit."

Consciousness is not the ether; the Universe as many teachings have shared nor does it reside inside the brain. The brain is an organ, just as the heart. The brain plays a part in creating conscious activity such as sight, sound response and physical conditions, however, it cannot operate on its own. It requires consciousness (awareness) to exist. And consciousness is knitted together with acknowledgement. We live in a shroud of unknowing purely because we do not recognise and do not <u>admit</u> the Superior that we ARE. We allow our conditioned thoughts to control our physical outcomes and have not admitted to ourselves and others that we are not a physical body, because we are a superior being, we are 'mind' and the mind is imagination. And we are here to play the physical game of life. Instead we disguise ourselves in external beliefs, and give these conditioned external beliefs the power of superiority.

Though we are identifiable as physical human beings, we are not definable. This means we are not limited and not explainable. We are incapable of being limited to definitions or beliefs. We cannot be explained because we are infinite and eternal, always changing and growing to new imagined experiences of the future. We are not a physical body, we create our physical body as we go and we do this by the beliefs that we hold either by unconditional choice or conditional choice. Whichever we give the power of dominion to.

<u>We are unlimited</u>. And it is the superior of us that needs to be acknowledged.

How do we believe this, especially with the layers of conditioned beliefs?

Most of us use a kettle to boil water. The components needed to boil water is the container/pot, a heating element, electricity, water, atmospheric pressure for the vapor pressure and gravity to keep the components from floating. The kettle is switched on, the water heats up and then it reaches the boiling point. Where is 'boiling'? It is identified as boiling, but we cannot define it or explain it exactly, because it cannot be specified, screened or isolated. We simply acknowledge the superior, 'boiling'. So where is 'life'? We have components such as organs, bones, tissues, chemicals, nutrients and breath. However, we cannot define or explain 'life,' where it occurs or how it appears when it is isolated. It is simply a sequence of Superior. Just as 'boiling' and 'life', 'mind' is unlimited, it cannot be wholly defined. Without Superior the kettle and body with all its components would not exist. And without imagination the 'mind' does not exist.

Conditioned beliefs are a language that divides us from our superior and our unique energy signature. This dividing from true self was passed on to each generation and it has broken our connection to ourselves and to acknowledging the superior within all others. We have become 'things', and we refer to each other in these words, for example; She is tall, he is rich, they are European, he is a lawyer, or I am a mother. Because of this we see the world as we describe it, as a divided assortment of 'things'.

We have also inherited judgement, what is right and what is wrong. We have judgements as to what looks good on a person, for example; someone thin looks better in a mini skirt and crop top rather than someone obese. And if an obese person was to wear it, we find many reasons as to why they should not wear it in public, such as; their fat is sticking out, it's ugly, outlandish or how dare they expose us to it. We even judge ourselves based on what is considered pretty, handsome, sexy, smart or healthy. We have judgements on what is ethical and moral. If someone takes something from us, by breaking into our home or vehicle, we would be very upset with this felon and perhaps relive this circumstance repeatedly, whether in our own minds or by sharing this unethical, unfair experience to others. All the while recreating these emotional frequencies over and over again asking the 'mind' to give us more experiences to make us feel angry, cheated, frustrated or judgemental.

What of an apple seed?

Here is the obvious. When an apple seed is planted it will grow to be an apple tree. It will grow branches, leaves and from these branches it will also produce apples.

If a person were to come along and pick an apple from this tree. The tree would not be upset or feel cheated because someone stole its apple. Nor would it feel devastated, believe itself to be broke or even bankrupt if someone were to pick off all the apples. If a tree lopper came along and chopped all the branches, down to a stump, the tree would not judge itself to be unappealing, useless and become depressed. Or feel the tree lopper is the master and abides by remaining as a stump. Instead, this apple tree will BE. BE the seed of an apple, one that can create more branches, leaves and apples. It will grow stronger, thicker and bushier. And produce more apples than before.

The apple tree is not a 'thing'. We have given it this title. It does not create through judgement in believing other trees to be better or worse. Nor does it believe itself to be anything other than what it is, a Superior that continues to produce more apples, branches, leaves, offshoots and more seeds. And always staying true to its unique energy signature, the creator of apples. You too are akin to the apple seed. You are not a 'thing.' A title, or a title who wears many hats. You have within you the ability and power to produce more than the apple tree. In fact, you can produce many kinds of fruit because apple is from *æppel,* meaning, "any kind of fruit."

Back to the example of a felon breaking into a home as stated in the previous paragraph. What is their experience and why did they do it? They could possibly just be an asshole, needed to get out of debt or something to sell for their next drug purchase. Or... they have practiced conditioned behaviours and are not aware of the Superior within.

What we experience in reality we give a definition to. We only require awareness, awareness of the divisions we make through our conditioned language, our conditioned beliefs. We have forgotten that our true self is Superior, each one of us. And that all we need to do is turn to ourselves for the answers. We have come to believe that what we see, what we touch, smell or hear is real. This has only placed a cloud of unknowing over our unique energy signature and as we continue to only believe in what is outside of us we confine our ability, giving ourselves useless boundaries and limits.

"Tell me to what you pay attention and I will tell you who you are."- *Jose Ortega y Gasset*

"When I see myself in others, I have no enemy." - *Juno Cristi*

"We are addicted to our thoughts. We cannot change anything if we cannot change our thinking." - *Santosh Kalwar*

I, Imagine

How many desires can fill an hour?

We can have as many desires as there are books in a library. And this is completely natural because within us we contain the entire knowledge of the universe, however, we only respond to our influenced and practised impulses. And a vast majority of us live only as clones, offshoots of our environment raised by these influences, unaware of our unique energy signature, and the simplicity in removing limitations.

Thought is imagination and it is the essence for creating our physical existence, at all times. Life outcome is transmitted through imagination by choice and decision. The code and the activator. A single thought is the bar code transmitted to the Universe or *"the formless substance - A thinking stuff that forms all things."* as Wallace Wattles calls it in his book, *"The Science Of Getting Rich,"* This transmitted bar code will give evidence of the exact product.

Choice is thought we give our attention to or what we believe to be true, the bar code of the product. If we extend this thought, we have decided to activate this in the thinking stuff, formless substance and bring to fruition the product (outcome) into our life. It can be joy, a touchable item, a feeling, fear or doubt. Even fear and doubt is a decision. Many of our thoughts we play over and over again in our minds. The more we repeat them we make the decision to reinforce specific thought patterns and welcome them into our life results again and again. Good or bad, we get what we decide every time.

In any moment, we can change our thought patterns regardless of how much we have repeated them and relieve ourselves from our restrictive beliefs and decisions. Einstein stated;

"The only reason for time is so that everything doesn't happen at once."

Everything cannot happen at once. Choose one pattern, one frequency. To feel healthy instead ill, safe instead of concern, or happy instead of anything you don't feel great about. All we need do is to make a decision, not analyze how we are feeling, or want to feel, this is only adding resistance if we overthink good or bad. Then follow it with a distraction to change the frequency. This could be to hum, jump around or get the DVDs out and put on a comedy.

Or you could imagine…

We are not limited to only thinking about what we desire. Even playing with our imagination, producing ideas of what is not present or has not been experienced will change the frequency transmitted to the formless substance and break any patterns that do not feel good. If we think of a cat. How it sleeps, eats and plays, it will change the frequency!

Allow yourself to Imagine. Use this word often. Because it is in this word that a mystery and one of the secrets is hidden.

From our environments such as school and media we have a conditioned belief installed. We do not see imagining as a real task. And this is a window of no resistance, no opposing. When we begin to transmit new thoughts and beliefs our critical mind will debate with doubts or fears such as; you can't do this, or what if something bad happens. These doubts and fears stem from conditioned beliefs that were shared to us by others in our environments and we heard it many times. The critical mind can be stronger, interrupt and oppose our desired thoughts, however, they can be surpassed by repetition of new beliefs, our 'why' and when we 'imagine'. We were never conditioned to believe 'imagine' to be a threat. Seeded beliefs have been shared with us for generations where we conclude the act of 'imagine' to be just a mind-game of fantasy, an unbelievable and artificial action. It is this seeded belief that gives to us a window of opportunity. The critical mind has no power of 'imagine' because the critical mind accepts 'imagine' as 'not real' and therefore the critical mind will not respond.

Think and speak the words 'I imagine'. When we do this we bypass the critical part of the mind and we enter though the back door of the imagination. Advertising experts know this. When we hear or see the word 'imagine' we respond to the product or service, and within our imagination we are thinking of various reasons why it would be great to have it and we believe what's on offer to be praiseworthy.

We all have the natural ability to imagine, and through this practice we awaken the sleeping giant, our unconditional, unlimited thought. You too, are an advertising expert, you respond well to any product you create in your mind. Use the word 'imagine' and take yourself on a journey to a new frequency.

Back to my rocking horse story:

I had no experience in woodworking nor had I ever used power tools. I thought of these tools as dangerous gadgets because I had heard people say they were dangerous and these were not contraptions for a woman, they were a man's toy. To me they were weapons of mass destruction that only professionals can use without cutting off a finger or doing some kind of physical damage. All I had was my why. I was doing this for my daughter and my reasoning at the time made sense. My mind was expanding and it was exciting. I knew I too could learn to become the professional (safely keeping all my body parts and eliminate any possibility of a possessed power tool wreaking havoc on my home, like an acme product in the road runner cartoons that always backfired on the coyote). And believed, without a doubt, that I could achieve this creation.

I began to imagine...Unconditioned thinking began to sprout, vivid unconditional belief that I can do it and I explored ways to build it. I wrote, I sketched plans, I worked out the materials and tools needed to accomplish my goal. I was excited, I was foreseeing the pleasure it would bring to my daughter and the joy I would personally gain from this experience. The more I focused, the more my ideas expanded, I had a list of ideas filling up my future agenda.

I soon discovered that when a thought is triggered and through the incredible power of a decision, followed by action, even the smallest step of writing it down will lead the way in achieving the result, our goal!

I had already decided within my thoughts that I was giving it my best shot; and this activated within the formless substance bringing to me more ideas, possibilities and opportunities to create the best rocking horse ever. I certainly had doubts along the way, my critical mind insisted on interrupting, but my why and my new beliefs kept me on the path to becoming a woodworking toymaker- and began my journey to self-rediscovery.

My independent action in building a rocking horse was completed. Only to discover I had made the mistake of gluing the head to the rear and the tail to the neck. It wasn't obvious though, it simply looked like a muscle horse with a large chest and smaller bottom, yet my daughter loved it and so did I, which was all that mattered (it was the best rocking horse ever to us). I enjoyed watching her play with it. The fulfillment of my imagination fueled hers. She played for hours and many years to come, role playing in her happy world of horse riding through forests and supermarkets (according to my daughter we ride horses down aisles). I even tried it out myself and we played together often.

"It doesn't matter what's happening... what matters is how you touch it."- *Nirmala*

Unshackle the Giant Within

Dear reader,

Are you discontented, dissatisfied with areas of your life? Do you desire something better? Harmonious relationships, financial security or ideal health? Why do you tolerate a standard existence? I have provided you with an intimate friend, a soul sensation; discontentment. And this intimate friend signals when your physical experiences do not match your unique desires. A reminder that your true happiness and purpose is yet to be attained and that you are capable of something more than an existence of subservience to others opinions. It will inspire you into action when you realise you are meant to be, do and have more. Your inheritance is waiting within reach for you to choose the bequests already gifted to you. I look forward to speaking with your unique self. Come visit me in your imagination.

Much love, from your inner self

In Xanadu did Kublai Khan a stately pleasure-dome decree, where Alph, the sacred river ran through caverns measureless to man down to a sunless sea. - *Kubla Khan By Samuel Taylor Coleridge-*

Just as Kubla Khan we are in Xanadu. A place of great beauty, luxury, and contentment, the Quantum field. The field of all possibilities. Our imagination resides in Xanadu. We cannot see it. It is sunless to the naked eye, however, within and without you is true self, your essence, your mind. A river flowing through infinite caverns of the Universe, the formless substance. An everlasting world full of beauty, luxury and contentment where you eternally emit the frequency of your dream to make it real, in your physical plane when you choose it. It is through inspiration and imagination that we create in Xanadu and it is here we can play with the game of life, having anything we desire. There is separation shackled in your thoughts, beliefs that limit the abundance that is within your reach. Beliefs that serve you only in lack and veil your opportunities to your pleasure dome. It's time for your giant within to emerge.

Albert Einstein is probably the best known scientist of the 20th Century and mostly known of his famous equation $E=mc^2$. Yet Einstein left many clues on the topic of the imagination. Einstein stated: *"I am enough of an artist to draw freely upon my imagination. Imagination is more important than knowledge. The true sign of intelligence is not knowledge but imagination. Knowledge is limited. Imagination encircles the world".* Einstein also stated, *"Look deep into nature, and then you will understand everything better."* Inspiration can be found, not only in the words we read but, through our own eyes by how we choose to see our world.

We are a 'thinking being'. To exist in the physical world, we require two things. Our brain needs the body to create activity, the body needs the environment to create conscious activity. A body without an environment, like a brain without a body, ceases to function. Not only does this mean that the environment is connected directly to the essence of us through the body, it also means that essence is connected directly to the environment. Therefore, we can find inspiration in the environment, our physical world. Everything in our physical world is nature, creation is nature, trees, animals, technology, material items or people. Inspiration builds inspiration and inspiration sparks imagination.

It is when we allow our imagination to flow that ideas begin to stream into our incredible minds regardless of age, experience, and our circumstances; whether from the past or our present life.

There is a giant within you, within all of us, our unconditional, unlimited imagination, and the power you contain simply needs to be inspired.

If you could have anything, what would you choose on your wish making spree? What would you have chosen as a child? Perhaps there was a goal that you had in mind. A road not yet taken, a treasure to find, a gift to develop, a journey to take, or maybe a change that you were hoping to make.

When we were children we believed in possibilities with no fear, no what ifs and no comparisons to cloud our judgment. We grow in age but in essence we are still that person, the dreamer, the hoper, the fireman, rock star, dancer, artist, policeman, adventurer or inventor of our future.

Inventor: c. 1500, "a discoverer, one who finds out, contriver, author, proposer, founder."

We are the authors and founders of our future!

As the years continue we truly are fortunate to have been gifted with a multitude of experiences, yet it is our conditioned beliefs that guide us as to how we view these experiences and how our lives pan out.

Remember this? When I grow up I'm going to ……….. (Fill in this gap).

As we continue to think, act and do as we have been conditioned, the visual memories of our childhood or belief in our own potential become sparse in our clouded adult mind. And it is the thinking that slumbers that drove our boundless, childlike, immense imagination.

Our success, dreams and happiness are dependent on one simple answer. Make it your own! Your experiences are being created by you each and every moment, on automatic from your habitual patterns, your conditioned beliefs. The beliefs that brought to you your past and current situations. You have the power to change anything, anytime and as soon as you make the decision to reign over your conditioned beliefs you have altered the frequency for new personalised and rewarding ones to be created.

Daily we all carry with us the tremendous mental faculty, our imagination. And as Albert Einstein stated, *"The true sign of intelligence is not knowledge but imagination"*. Imagination has its own personal assistant - inspiration (c. 1300, "immediate influence of God, inhaling, breathing in, breathe upon."). God, from PIE *ghut- "that which is invoked."

Inspiration is found everywhere! Everything in creation. Our family, friends, and people we observe or others we hear about. Animals, elements, technology, gardens, music, all non-physical and physical objects; and all provide a boundless supply of inspiration for the imagination. Use your vivid imagination for your new future. Say this out aloud: I am a GIANT of possibilities! Because, you have the power!

We can begin a story from factual information and stretch this to pure invention through our own eyes. Whether it be tangible items or an intangible belief. Invention is the result of imagination.

Through invention our imagination gives us the ability to form mental images of things that are not physically present, have never been conceived or created and to distort or innovate things that are physically present. The more we practice invention by repetition we will discover it begins to turn into habit. This habit grows, our repertoire of inspiration also grows and our imagination begins to create an endless stream of ideas.

When it comes to literature, readers have a preferred genre, such as; fantasy, romance, science fiction, crime stories, humour, adult fiction, young adult fiction, paranormal, mystery and this list goes on; while some readers enjoy variety. My chosen path in fictional books is aimed for children and the young at heart. I enjoy fantasy and humor. Through repetition of invention my imagination formed a habit for these genres.

When I unleashed my imagination and accepted it as part of who I am I began by observing or listening to my surroundings. I stopped and focused, even for a few seconds and allowed myself to invent possibilities during my quiet moments of unconditional thought. I exercised my mental muscles, they strengthened, and my dendrites grew. This habit grew to become a natural part of my days, and I now have the ability to see and invent possibilities, fact or fiction, regardless of any distraction.

Let me invent some fiction examples right now:

Science tells us of Microbial Discoveries. Minute life forms known as microorganisms. These microbes cannot be seen with the naked eye and can only be observed through a microscope.

These microbial creatures are all around us and if added to and viewed through the lense of perception; of what we have been taught, our beliefs, fears, things we like, things we love or even our observations of people, we can create a unique storyline.

I'll pick an inanimate object for this one. Let's say a street sign.

I am driving, heading towards my destination and looking at the street names. As I pass the signs I spot one and the street is called Brussel Street, the suburb is Northlakes, Brisbane. I look at the surroundings of this sign and notice the steel pole housing the street sign is embedded in the soil covered with manicured grass.

I am aware of microbes and that they can be found on an inanimate object.

To my imagination, the street sign becomes the city of Brussel (not to be confused with Brussels in Belgium), I pull over and note my observations, I can feel a story coming on.

Sometimes it is just the words, sounds or observations that I note and other times I might elaborate. It solely depends on what I am doing at the time and what my schedule is like.

Now I know there is a city called Brussel, but what of the other observations. Microbes become characters and it is how I personally see them through the lense of experiences; my upbringing, what I have read or what I have learnt in my life, that I begin to perceive them as sweet, frightening, grotesque or comical.

I have two character names already Northlakes and Brisbane. The steel pole becomes the culture.... Northlakes and Brisbane of the Steeling tribe live in the city of Brussel.

What of the manicured grass...well...This can be a completely new city filled with green spiked buildings with more microbe characters or insects.

Now, you may be thinking how does this fictional story help me with real life?

Well, you can create fiction anyway you choose. A small home can become a mansion or the guest house of an estate. Ill health can become your body simply telling you to have a moments rest because you over exerted yourself during a mountain climbing expedition. A person you see in the street steps into a car you desire can become your chauffeur taking the car to another parking location. Or if it is cold winters day, you could imagine the snow outside of the cabin you are vacationing in. Whatever you choose to invent including fantasy, romance, humour, or any other genre you apply, through repetition of invention your imagination will form the habit. And this habit will transmit your decision into the formless substance bringing to you the results, the frequency that will match how you felt whilst you lived in the imagination.

Everything around us has the potential of inspiration. Delve into anything you have attained from childhood. Have an active interest in life, the world around you, particularly in people, how they live, what they think and how they behave. You can relate to the life of anyone and expand it to suit your happiness. Stop, observe, and see where your imagination will carry you, even a small change or invention can allow your imaginings to grow into an enormous idea.

Allow it to be something that intrigues you, drives you or something you become passionate about and the passion will flow. Any idea, anything that inspires us is *wunderfoll* because they are the stimulant that feeds our imagination, which inspires and motivates our mind.

This stimulant still needs an added ingredient. The ingredient which assists with decision and action. The 'WHY'. Your 'why!' Inspiration ignites the flame within each and every person, as opposed to motivation, which is doing something that we don't really want to do yet if we persist we will achieve it. This is not in harmony with our true desires. We do not need to convince ourselves to keep going. Our why gives us a clear picture of what we want, what we want to experience and what makes us feel good. In 1995 my 'why' began with doing something for my daughter, I wanted to build her a rocking horse. I had watched her play on the little merry-go-round horses and she loved it. She pointed out horses in picture books and she loved them. I wanted her to have her own horse to play with and give myself the opportunity to watch her enjoyment, this thought made me happy. This urge led me to action and though to me it was an unknown path, the 'why' kept my decision alight.

Find your why and release the fantastic flow to expand in your mind. Enjoy the creations that will stream from the festival of your imagination. It could be for a family member or simply because you want happiness. It could purely be that you love the idea, it's your reasoning. Find your why and the path to your new life.

"A dream is in the mind of the believer and in the hands of the doer. You are not given a dream without being given the power to make it come true." —*Anonymous*

Part II
WHO WAS I?

Conditioned Tempering

Are You In Control Of Your Life?

From birth we are taught by theories. A group of ideas about how something should be done, made, or thought about from our environment. Which includes relations, community, audio, visual and all contact. Our interpretation of what we hear, see, smell, touch and taste as we grow is influenced by systematic arrangements from an immense network of experiences, and passed down from generations, known Conditioned Tempering.

There are many mentors or life coaches who often use the word 'paradigm.' For many years I'd never heard this word, nor did I know what it meant. At first I thought it only meant some beliefs; such as superstitions, however, I learned that this word was commonly used as a definition for patterned beliefs. Yet when I delved deeper I discovered this was not the word to awaken awareness. There was a deeper understanding that needed to surface. And it is knowing how we got to where we are.

Conditioned: from *condicion,*" to stipulate, state, behave, social status"

Tempering: from *temprian,* " to moderate, bring to a proper or suitable state, to modify some excessive quality, to restrain within due limits."

Conditioned Tempering is our copied patterns, ways of thinking; our habits, modelled concepts, frameworks of assumptions and our belief in limits.

It is the conditional (modified and restrained) education (a rearing, training) we have rooted from birth to now from our entire environment that has tempered with our true identity. Conditioned Tempering governs our thoughts, our ideas, denotes our responses, patterns of behavior and makes us predictable. And the BIG one, these are the transmissions to the formless substance which give us our outcomes.

When I became aware of this, it led me to observe myself, my habitual behavior, as well as my environment.

As we grow we can become trapped in a foundation mindset. Our minds become simply a storage device for memorisation of our influencing environment and we continue in our ways following these teachings and influences, without question and yet occasionally, quietly in our thoughts we intuitively sense that there could be other possibilities.

We have unanswered questions and somehow know there is more to the meaning of life than what we have been conditioned to believe. We have obvious questions, for example; why is there still so much ill health when we live in such an advanced age of medical technology or with an education system that has improved since the early 20th century, why is it that more and more children across the globe are struggling to read? What of the Pyramids? There are many theories and hearsays, yet we are still no wiser as to the truth behind the mysteries. And foods! Eat this, it's healthy… then months later another discovery to say No! don't eat that, eat this instead. Eat three times a day. No! Eat five small meals. Don't eat after this time. Drink a glass of water before meals because… Don't drink a glass of water before meal because… Don't…Do…Don't… Do… It's no wonder why poor mental health has increased in Western Society due to the Information Age pouring out data overloads of confusion, contradiction and vagueness.

The overload of data and belief principles have aided in disguising our immense possibilities, helping us forget that our true identity contains and IS unconditioned and unconditional thought.

Not…conditioned, Not…conditional!

Not… limited by conditions regardless of our environments, the beliefs and cultural practices.

We ARE… unrestricted by conditions.

We only truly ARE …infinite, absolute and <u>WITHOUT LIMITATIONS!</u>

Our unconditioned, unlimited thoughts are shrouded; overlapped and conditioned by concepts and opinions of what is right or wrong, what is good or bad, what looks good, what sounds good, what feels good and what adult behavior is, for example; an adult dreamer is not being responsible, therefore in adult life we abide by what is expected and dismiss what is the supposed immature thinking. We block ourselves off from our childhood dreams, we accept without challenge that our influenced ideas are rational and convince ourselves, 'this is right, we're grownups now'. And we, just as others shared with us, pass on our conditioned beliefs to our children, friends, work colleagues or anyone we meet, all the while giving aide in shrouding them from their immense possibilities and true identity.

What is an opinion?

From Latin *opinionem*, "a fancy."

An opinion is the imagination, a fancy and any opinion only becomes real if we attach belief to it.

Attachment to something/s physical and non-physical such as; people, emotions or items only carries with it a definition, a belief. For example; we have known each other for years therefore they should understand me. I have invested a lot of money in this, John did and made a million. It comes in threes, something else is going to happen. I feel stressed because I have too much to do. I have a headache because I didn't sleep well. Nothing goes my way, he/she gets all the luck. Or the common one; that's my car (or thing, person, status).

My, me or mine are automatic responses to fear and lack. It carries disguised conditioned thoughts of 'what if something happens' to my, me or mine as well as 'just in case'. We claim ownership and act in ways to protect what belongs to us and transmit thoughts of 'I just want this only or am unable to get more'. Definitions including disguised thoughts, are attachments. They are only beliefs and will add limitations to our experiences in life. And these attachments will create our life outcome.

Beliefs are always based on very few facts. There is always a degree of doubt about a belief. If one defends a belief, they have doubt, and ironically this is disbelief. Otherwise they would be at peace just knowing it to be true regardless of what another debates. Knowing something to be true needs no proof, convincing or words. It is a simple feeling from within that gives a sensation of warmth and contentment. If we gained beliefs through studies of books, audios or from other people, this is still only very few facts. This shared information is already tainted with conditioned and conditional thoughts. We even read and listen through our conditioned thoughts. After all there are many books, audios and varied opinions on any and the same subject. Which one is true? When we try to prove our beliefs we are actually trying to prove our decision to believe it. The real need is to be right.

We are souls, unique energy signatures always in the process of advancing and gaining wisdom as we move through each day, each week, and each year of our life. When something really is true, we feel it, there is a calmness within us and have no need to explain. This is knowingness and listening to our self. This is wisdom.

We live in an ever changing, ever evolving world yet we continue to carry beliefs that for many do not apply, such as fears of snakes, spiders and rats. Have you ever died from these bites and been resurrected? Have you ever caught a disease from a mouse or rat? We also carry beliefs, inventions from numerous years ago, that do not apply in the 'now', beliefs such as; 'saving for rainy day'. A belief that was invented during hardship and in an age of depression. Times that did not contain the abundance we have around us today.

We 'now' have food that is easily accessible, organizations that help those in need, services to guide us in our requirements, physical stores and the internet to attain anything we require, cheaper and faster than times ago. Yet we still hold onto 'things' and 'save for rainy day,' for example; left over food, dinnerware, furniture, electronics or fill our cupboards with clothing from sales. Sales that occur not only every five years but often throughout each year. Some of these things we hold onto are chipped, torn, broken and are in need of repair, of which we will get to 'one day'.

These thoughts of lack and limitation we choose to believe are transmitting to the formless substance from which all things are made. We ask to make more of; 'give me fear, I want more broken things and I'm saving for a rainy day because I cannot do it later, I will be incapable in the future.' As you ask so shall you receive.

My conditioned tempering:

I had been so encompassed by my conditioned and conditional beliefs. I was taught how to act and think, what was expected of me, to be the responsible adult, the good housewife, the perfect parent and believed I was content with the concept of conformity and the white picket fence that I never allowed a space in my mind for thinking beyond my box.

Even my journey as a woodworking toymaker was interrupted many times with thoughts of what I had been conditioned to believe; women don't do certain things, it's a man's job, how am I really going to get ahead, building a rocking horse is a waste of time when there are other more important things. I had to think of the bills, getting ahead, stop wasting time or money, what if I got sick and I should be 'saving for a rainy day'. I had family members and friends saying; you'll burn yourself out, she doesn't need a rocking horse or you don't know how to do it. But my new founded purpose and why ignored the mind chatters as well as the advice given with good intention from those who cared for me. My conditioned thoughts were losing the battle; I was learning to follow my own unconditional thoughts. Questions I asked myself returned answers that at many times were nonsensical such as "you'll burn yourself out". How? When I was enjoying this idea and planning, I had more energy than ever, I felt healthy and more importantly, I was happy. I continued to listen to my 'Self'.

"The question is how the questioner exists." - *Kedar Joshi*

"Wisdom is the reward you get for a lifetime of listening when you'd have preferred to talk." - *Doug Larson*

Impress or Distress

Impress: from *impressus,* "have a strong effect on the mind or heart, to stamp deeply in the mind."

Distress: from *destresse.,* "circumstance that causes anxiety or hardship."

The years following 1995, as stated earlier, I was clueless that my habitual ways were breaking. I enjoyed many of the new experiences that presented in my life. My daughter and I were happy and our health was ideal. I was approached with a job offer that led me to teach art and crafts, as well as a floristry class for a technical college. I had no credentials, only word of mouth from those who saw the abilities I expressed. This paid well even though it was only two days each week, and I earned more than enough money to decorate our home for comfort. I was offered another position as a property officer in Co-operative housing and this led me to designing and drafting for residential, retail and commercial premises. As the old saying goes, "things just fell into my lap".

People were giving me clues, unbeknownst to them, as to why I had been doing so well and why things were working out for me. "How do you do it? You're so lucky! You have a great imagination! How do you get your ideas? I want some of what you're on!"

For many years these words were foreign to me and if for some reason I was asked such things, I saw it as an insult. I was conditioned to believe that a great imagination was not part of my life and that those who powered up their imaginations were only children, drunks or addicts such as Jimmy Hendrix, the influential electric guitarist, singer and songwriter or Arthur Conan Doyle's famous detective Sherlock Holmes.

I was a responsible adult and a mum, especially when I became a single mum. I had seventy-five cents to my name, broken bones, no home, no furniture, not even a coffee cup; what I did have was a toddler that I needed to provide for, and there was no way I was wasting my time on menial notions like the imagination. I had to stay focused, be mature, and work out ways to live, pay expenses and hopefully get ahead one day!

However, it was in these expressions, these clues given by others that indicated the 'how'. How I found the key to open the treasure chest of possibilities and the simple route to my successful package. I was ignorant in noticing what they were really referring to was my ability, even by fluking it, to overcome and surpass many conditioned beliefs. I was believing new perceptions, I believed I had a great imagination, my ideas were worthy and that lady luck was on my side.

Reflect on your past and recall a time when your life experience was happy or 'lucky'. The rocking horse experience in later years was an indicator. I was able to recognise 'why' great things were coming my way. It never was lady luck. It was the thought patterns I held to be true. I received because, fundamentally I believed good things were possible. The words 'lady luck' simply meant 'good things' to me. And good things expanded in the imagination brings more good things. We are transmitters to the formless substance, now and we transmitted in the past. Recall an experience that was great for you; and this will demonstrate your thought patterns, giving you the opportunity to recognise your 'how'. How you too had great things coming your way.

My project to build a rocking horse was the catalyst to my successes. My action and 'why' became the stimulant that impressed a new belief. The belief that I could do it, regardless of the experience, knowledge and influences surrounding me. Had I not found myself a project that gave me a burning desire for my 'why', I could have possibly drowned in a pool of my conditioned beliefs and followed the path of victim, living only to blame others. My excitement and activity prevented this. And each moment whether it was researching, planning, sketching, collecting items or construction of the rocking horse, my imagination was resuscitated, and inspiration bred more inspiration. Find your 'why' and move towards new beliefs that will serve your desired outcomes in life.

There are three Universal Laws that were at play when I chose to become a woodworker. I wasn't aware of them at the time, however, these Laws were put into action and in return gave me wonderful results. They are:

The Law of Self-Knowledge: One who does not know himself, having never tested himself or his limitations does not know what he can do.

You must know yourself. See the value in yourself and this will lead to a greater sense of the flow in all of life. - The 30 Laws of Flow, Charlene Day

"If you do not conquer self, you will be conquered by self."- Napoleon Hill

The Law of Non-Resistance- When we resist a condition, person, or thing that we don't like or want, we are adding power to it. Resistance keeps us stuck. Non-resistance allows us to go free. (I did not like power tools, but this did not stop me.)

Learn to respond rather than react. Learn how to relax and go with the flow and be in acceptance. Stay focused on the real objective instead of being in resistance. - The 30 Laws of Flow, Charlene Day

Resistance is a signal that you are moving into a new area, however, whatever you resist persists. Do not resist." - Bob Proctor

The Law of Action: Action that supports your desires allows you to bring to fruition things on earth and get the results you want. Action is definitely a key to success.

"In order to carry a positive action we must develop here a positive vision." - Dalai Lama

A few simple shifts in habit and beliefs can also tip the scales, starting the path towards abundance. We can restart or reset our experience anytime just by playing with inspiration and this will open new paths to imaginary possibilities. These shifts can also alter our DNA.

We are told that our eye colour, height, health conditions and mental states are all influenced by our DNA. However, the science of epigenetics (study of the process by which genetic information is translated into the substance and behavior), shows us that all this can be altered through magnetic fields, heart coherence, positive mental states and intention. Many have believed that the DNA determines who we are and what will become. Researchers have shown through extensive studies that epigenetics entails DNA and based upon the places where we live, the climate around us, our thoughts, intentions, our emotions, and how we believe, all influence and can alter the outcomes of each individual's DNA blueprint.

Change your habits; the internal environment, your thoughts and beliefs, it will change your external environment; and this results in new DNA, and…An alteration in the genes. Segments of DNA molecule are called genes (genes are made of DNA). We are never governed by the conditions, illnesses or results of our parents and ancestors. We CAN live in or often visit a physical environment that supports the outcomes we desire. We CAN change our conditioned beliefs and set intentions with goals to suit what we uniquely want. If we feel bad, we CAN reset our emotions anytime by walking about, humming or form any action to change the frequency. We HAVE THE ABILITY to alter our genes anytime we choose and to become our unique self.

We don't need an illogical or fictitious reason (or better yet a mind altering substance) for living with a great imagination. Our imagination can assist in shifting our habits. Our Imagination is our companion to infinite possibilities. And it's our friend forever always ready to take us wherever we choose.

"I think, therefore I am." — *René Descartes*

"Everything changes when you start to emit your own frequency rather than absorbing the frequencies around you, when you start imprinting your intent on the universe rather than receiving an imprint from existence." — *Barbara Marciniak*

The evasive clone carousel

"I've been to paradise, but I've never been to me." - Charlene

Lack of awareness and conditioned tempering, matters not, they are still decisions made by us in the eyes of the Universe. Our automatic (performed without conscious thought) decisions each and every day are shaping our futures. We are creating our health conditions, wealth results and relationship outcomes with the beliefs we hold in these choices. And this keeps us riding on the merry-go-round of our chosen life. We are the offshoot, the branches of our environments, and lack of awareness in ourselves allows this merry-go-round to continue its spiral and escape with our identity.

We unquestionably – though usually not without complaint – wake up in the morning, whether it be by alarm clock or body clock, to routinely prepare for going to work or household duties. Our conditioned operating routines, day in and day out, along with our beliefs, keep us busy, distracted and – for some – overwhelmed into a clouded life.

I ask this… have you ever tried to force yourself to sleep? Perhaps you have an early workday or a job interview, a medical appointment, or maybe an important event that requires punctuality. Your alarm clock is set for 5 a.m. and you still lay awake at 11 p.m., concerned, glancing at the clock, thinking, "Argh, I have six hours to go before I get up." Regardless of your thoughts to get to sleep you lay awake, though you insist on keeping your eyes closed, only opening them to glimpse at the clock, and you calculate again. "Argh, four hours before I have to wake up," you think, and anxiety begins to rear its ugly head. This game can continue over the next few hours, even days. Noises become apparent; pillows feel uncomfortable; and your body may feel discomfort, maybe pain, or decides it requires a few trips to the bathroom for relief.

When we compare us to the natural world it is quite profound how we are very much alike. On the surface we appear to be different, however, there is a key component that separates us humans from the rest of the natural world. We have well developed, ingrained conditioned thoughts and beliefs that gets in the way of opportunity; and can keep us looking at that damn clock, worrying about sleeping in or being tired the next day.

The more I observed the natural world, the more I gained insight into how nature can adapt quite well, regardless of what their ancestors did or what is assumed to be the ideal way for all types of flora or fauna to behave. Nature flows and evolves with change. It moves on with little effort and flourishes.

We build suburbs from bricks, concrete or steel, yet plants will grow in strange places such as roof gutters, brick, or concrete walls. They will grow out of the smallest crack in the footpath, even in steel structures. Some of these plants we call weeds. This is an interesting topic in itself. In Australia we have seven states. Each of these states have definitions as to what constitutes a weed, for example: in Victoria, agapanthus is considered to be obnoxious weeds, yet in other states they are sort after and considered quite beautiful. In Queensland it is lantana, yet in other states and other countries such as New Zealand people adorn their homes with these. There are many countries that eat what we in Australia call weeds as well as utilize the leaves or flowers for tea. Weeds are only a weeds because of what we are taught, and it is a definition that creates belief within us, becoming another conditioned thought added to the layers we already carry within our minds.

Weeds are one of our greatest teachers! They choose to grow and flourish their own way. They do not grow in rows or follow what other plants do, nor attempt at being another plant on the assumption that another is better, stronger or lovelier. Every singular weed presents diverse differences from the next. No leaf is the same shape and size to the other, and each leaf has different patterns and combinations of lines. They do not follow trends of the era or in the footsteps of their parent plant from where they seeded, unlike us. They take the opportunity to be their unique self, to live by their own soul print, to grow where they choose, how they choose and what is best for them in the given moment.

Just as a soul print exists in the natural world it exists with each and every person. It is the uniqueness of each one of us, much like our thumb print. What is ideal for another is not ideal for the next. This is why we experience such things as yearning, frustration, depression or anger. When we live our experiences by conditioned tempering we are riding the clone carousel, the merry-go-round of other people's life outcomes and blocking our soul print, our unique energy signature. Stuck in a prison of automatic unwanted experiences.

This unique energy signature is what a person is

born to realise. To discover who they are and who they are not. We are also given a unique gift from the Universe and this is our gift we return to the Universe. A gift of expansion for tomorrow and years to come. Expansion of new ideas, new experiences, new sensations, new services and a host of these inventions are to be found within the imagination.

When we become aware of our conditional behavior and mental conditionings, we begin to unshroud the patterns of beliefs and opinions; this enables us to find the answers within. It would be wrong of me to give an example of what ones soul print could be. I would be planting a seed within the imagination and only help in creating more conditioned tempering. Nobody can do this for you, it is the journey only for the individual.

Our essence, our soul, does not speak to us in words. It speaks to us through dreams, intuition, urges, and physical sensations. We have cluttered our thoughts with beliefs and opinions; and when a message comes we miss it, or dismiss it with excuses, interpretations and distractions from external events.

Begin to listen to your body. The natural state of your soul is to feel good. If at any point you do not feel this, respond to how you feel. There is a defined belief and an emotional state making this connection and shrouding your way. You do not need to analyze how you feel, this will only add attachment to your state. Just recognise the feeling and move to a distraction. Something that actually makes you feel good. In any moment you have the power of decision to do this. You have unlimited thought. The more you practice this the closer you get to clearly hearing your soul's voice.

There are many beliefs and definitions that exist in our world, and though there are some that resonate, working well for our happiness, there are many that disempower the self when left to govern our lives without question or change. A person is unable to flourish completely if they only follow what the other is doing, following another's soul print only creates resistance, a battle or blocks to the one who lives without self-actualization.

Many are unaware that our mind, body and circumstances are simply an outcome of ideas and patterned beliefs we hold in our minds. We, through choice can see ourselves as having ideal health, youthfulness and longevity rather than beliefs of disease, old age and death. To believe these conditionings is to carry out their orders and bring to fruition the results of these one-sided beliefs. There is a vast amount of evidence where time seems to stand still for some. They are youthful in appearance, have vitality and wellness well past the age of eighty. There are even some that do not eat 'healthy foods' yet are themselves healthy and slim. Our physiological body is designed to regenerate and survive, hence we have mechanisms, such as; immunity and ways of expelling what does not aid in the regeneration. It is only the beliefs we hold of ill health, conditions and death that will deteriorate the ideal health we are all designed to have. Give yourself a new order; trust and surrender to the Divine design that is your inheritance, repeat this daily until you impress a new belief upon your mind;

"I express Divine design in my mind, body and outcomes, ideal, I am."

By repeating this statement, you will begin to notice the changes soon taking place, a chemical change will occur in your body, because new ideas and ideals will surpass your old beliefs, and by expanding your new beliefs of ideal health, youthfulness and longevity your physical self will change for the better. Remember everything has an opposite, ill health can be ideal health if you choose it to be.

Duplicating old patterns and beliefs is allowing others to do your thinking, to lead your way without question and to invite similar experiences over and over again. Bypass these opinions and engage directly with the source.

Go inward and connect to your accurate self, your own Divine potential. Your unconditioned, infinite, absolute, without limitations God-like self.

When you are feeling good this is your inner message or intuition saying you have reconnected to your true self. Intuition or 'gut instinct' is unconditioned response and a powerful tool we carry around with us, innately (from *innatus* "inborn, native, natural"), every day. We all have the ability to assess what is right or wrong, what feels good or bad. Take advice from your inner guidance, and choose what makes YOU feel good, your own desires rather than the influences, and conditioned beliefs of the backdrop that surrounds you now or yesterday. Reject some of your programmed beliefs and follow your unique greatness.

Our natural world has no use or need for what other natural elements believe and do. Plants just grow, maybe in some strange places but they still carry on, adapt to change and thrive. Animals and birds live and nest in strange places, too, yet they still continue to exist by creating what is best for them. They are not gifted with choice, like us. Beings granted with free will and the power to choose at any given moment. We have the choice to accept or disregard any conditioned belief. This point is so important, I'm going to repeat it, "We have the <u>choice</u> to accept or disregard any conditioned belief." Choice: from *ceosan*, "seek out, select opportunity from a number of opportunities; decide, test, taste, try; accept, approve". We only need to listen to ourselves, reconnect with our unconditioned selves and feel what is truly ideal for our individual self.

What is change? Change, is to make the form, nature, content or future course different from what it is or from what it would be, if left alone. If we do not see the value in change, we only get back the results of our past experiences. Experiences influenced by other people's conditioned thoughts and beliefs that were passed onto us, hence we replicate the lives of our families or ancestors, as well as customs in our environment, such as communities, advertising or professional opinion, professional opinion that often changes when there is a new discovery. And this is what creates our negative emotions, frustration, anxiety, depression, doubt, fear or low self-esteem because we are tuned in and follow the opinions of others without being accountable to our own soul print. If we neglect our individual soul print, we can never feel whole, and therefore miss the opportunity of true happiness.

Everything, as stated in a previous chapter, is simply a belief with an attached definition. There is a surplus of varied definitions for any belief including any word, as well as deeper meanings and understandings for each. We just have to look up a word in the assortment of dictionaries from origin right through to new age concepts to learn the overload of definitions. Beliefs, just as words over past years, have an been added to, altered or redefined many times. And with the cultural differences across the earth, beliefs have a variety of definitions during the same time. Which beliefs are right? The only right beliefs for you are the ones that uniquely makes you feel good.

Change is one of those words that have many interpretations and some of the common attachments to it are, "change can be hard or scary and I/he/she/they has fear of change." Keep in mind, however, that a belief is only an opinion, it was not real when it was created, and it began in the imagination. It is only created in our own beliefs if we choose to accept it as true.

When we experience sudden change some panic, stress and start thinking such things as; this is not right, this is not how it should be, why me, or why do these things happen, and this only results in us being stuck. Some are stuck like this for a long time. Stuck in a belief that we are powerless and believe there is something outside of ourselves that is the culprit or there is some external remedy that may be able to fix it.

Plants or animals change and adapt to the ever evolving environment. Why is that? Animals don't have conditioned beliefs, however, there are some species that do not flow with the changes and they come to be known as endangered. Many though view the opportunities around them. Opportunities they would not have considered had sudden change not occurred and move forward to thrive. They are free from the restraints of conditioned beliefs including what one does and thinks when an unexpected event occurs; or what is the appropriate procedure and behavior for moving forward towards success. Animals and birds will live in structures that are not considered natural. Our homes become their crevices; large buildings become mountains and caves; towers, power poles or street signs become trees. They change to a new opportunity and act in the moment to adapt in change; and unlike humans, they do not go out on revenge, depression or stay put. They do not hold onto the past and replicate or imitate previous behaviors; this will only lead to them becoming an endangered species. It is only us that see fault in change, whilst the fauna scurry, hop or fly around, harmonizing with the flow and being who they are.

The answer is all around us, yet life stops us from seeing it. Our jungle of ideas, our perception of what is important, our occupied days and swamped lives build on the turf of our conditioned thoughts and beliefs. And it is ironic when we discover, that many answers, are in life itself. It is every day and every moment that life exhibits this answer, in plain view. We look but we do not see. For example:

In Australia we have many kangaroos. It is not unusual to see some come out to the roads at twilight, particularly in the stretch of roads near the unpopulated areas. When a kangaroo sees a light they are blinded and start a hop toward this light, many a times we can find the carcass of a cold body spread on the side of a road, hit by the car which shone the light. We, or should I say, the driver and passengers of a vehicle, are startled, screech and panic upon impact from the strong body of a kangaroo. A sigh of relief emerges when they discover they have survived and though there is damage to the vehicle, lady luck was on their side.

What of the kangaroo? Lady luck was not on its side! It is a natural response for us to feel relief after such an event, we are ok, phew! We can feel pity for the deceased animal, some show emotion and release tears, then we continue, back on track, and journey to our destination.

What did we not see? We looked and ascertained that the body of the kangaroo, is now definitely in an eternal slumber. But, what did we miss?

We have responses through our conditioned beliefs. Had it been a human we would have acted in a different way, there would have been fear of manslaughter, devastation because it is a human life or thoughts of what went wrong, was there speeding, negligence, did this person cause it. Did we see life? What of the colony, waiting in the sidelines? Perhaps a mate, or a child, a joey. What if this departed kangaroo was the provider, the nurturer or the protector? What will now happen to the awaiting colony? We looked at the deceased body and feel a sense of ease because it's not manslaughter, it's not human after all, therefore, we see it as road kill. Did we see that the repercussion of our action should include a funeral? Perhaps not, because road kill is related to animals, and not a human. A funeral for road kill is not a conditioned belief, nor do we see road kill as a responsibility because many of us have conditioned views that the life of an animal is of lesser significance than the life of a human. Just as we do not see the repercussions of many conditioned actions, our beliefs create our biggest repercussions.

Everything we believe, every concept and word we have a definition to, has a repercussion. This example of the kangaroo seems extreme, yet, there are more acute repercussions for other actions we do and go through life with lack of awareness.

What of wealth? The dreaded or glorious concept of material wealth. Some attain it easily, some inherit it, and others reach the point of success only for a period of time until they return back to square one. Yet most work hard only to pay expenses hoping they don't fall into the black hole of pure poverty like the beggars they see on TV or the streets, living week to week with the concerns of bills and wishing for the day they get ahead.

Wealth, health and happiness depends upon our habitual beliefs. Ninety-five percent of our experiences, circumstances and the people in our lives occurs due to our conditioned thoughts and beliefs. We are on automatic, and our practiced thoughts are an automatic response, picking our transmissions and bringing our experiences for us. Whatever we have been exposed to in our environment and experienced through our senses; smell, touch, taste, hear and see, it has influenced our automatic pilot. We are and always will be a product of our environment. Clones with a data bank of beliefs installed from opinions of others.

Unless…

Have you stopped to think of what you truly want,

what is your purpose in this life? What if a job, alarm clocks, taxes, mortgages, rent or bills did not exist? What would you want? How would you exist? What would you create? What would you choose? When will you stop riding the evasive clone carousel?

Think of Mary Poppins, use your imagination. In the Disney movie, Mary, Bert, the chimney sweep, and the children, Jane and Michael, leapt onto a merry-go-round. Mary on a black horse and Bert on a grey. Bert says to Mary, "Very nice. Very nice, indeed, if you don't wanna go nowhere." Mary replies, "Who says we're not going anywhere? On, guard!" And they were off! They rode on their fairground horses to other opportunities, rescued a fox from a hunting party, hopped onto a race track, posed for photographers after Mary wins the race, and have a mingle with kings and queens. See how much happens once you get off the evasive clone carousel. Why, stay on the merry-go-round of conditioned beliefs? As Bert says, "Very nice. Very nice, indeed, <u>if you don't wanna go nowhere.</u>"

Our individual beliefs, the ideas passed onto us from generations before us, as well as our existing circumstances, have assisted and influenced us to become who we are and believe we have limits.

We accompany ourselves every day, yet many are still peering through hope or worse still defeat. Life gets in the way or so we think. We believe external occurrences, people or our lacks sometimes stops us from seeing or reaching our passions. While we mimic our influencers we think we have our own perception of what is important or what possibilities can be attained. These occupied days of life getting in the way, distracted lives and cloned perceptions build on the ever growing garden of our conditioned beliefs.

We accept the distractions of our everyday lives, and the routines we have come to believe as normal living. We work, pay bills, do hobbies, have a savings account, build on our assets and tend to household chores such as cleaning the additional furniture pieces and appliances we decorate our homes with. We live by other people's concepts, ideas planted into our own minds, think by using another's thought; all this time we hold these inventions from the imagination to be true and unknowingly walk through our lives riding the evasive clone carousel.

Our minds have been set into a habitual pattern of ideas and thoughts for us to live by and this relates to everything in our everyday living. Do you know your conditioned thoughts and beliefs? Are your choices and beliefs your own? Do all the sets of values and beliefs make sense to you? An example is superstition; seven years' bad luck for breaking a mirror. A mirror is a sheet of glass with a reflective film on the back, do you get seven years bad luck if you break glass? NO!

There are opportunities appearing every day and lessons for our personal unique growth. This life shows us how adaption and evolution can be in harmony when we overcome our mental conditionings and understand the effects of our habitual beliefs. Just as the kangaroos will now adapt to the sudden change in their minus one colony. We too can learn to adapt to change, walk a path by choice and never again accept only sustainability. Each one of us can thrive.

Reach out to yourself, assist yourself with one simple word that expresses your desire. A word you prefer and one that inspires you, for example; 'imagine'. A word that speaks volumes in possibilities. Permanently bind this word to your mind. This word becomes your shield and spear in combat and in peace. Use this word to beat upon every belief that no longer serves your desired outcomes and to force these beliefs down under a cloud of forgetting. Keep it intact, and the distractions of your mental conditionings will soon diminish.

As the conditioned thoughts and beliefs diminish, continue practicing, it becomes easier each time. This will remove clutter from the mind and gives freedom to be still. When you reach the point of stillness you open the window to hear your soul's voice and the opportunity to discover your unique energy signature.

"**Insanity**: doing the same thing over and over again and expecting different results." - *Albert Einstein*

"Just let awareness have its way with you completely." - *Scott Morrison*

"Nature does not deceive us; it is we who deceive ourselves." - *Jean-Jacques Rousseau*

"Faith is the daring of the soul to go farther than it can see"- *William Newton Clarke*

Subservient to whom?

Dear physical self,

You have limited skill and you offer no assistance. Be silent! Ignore the activity of your conditioned thoughts by devoutly turning within. If not, quite likely, you will imagine your ideas are helpful. Many excellent and wonderful aspects spring up in your mind. They appear positive and worthy of your consideration, but as the mental chatter continues, it drags you down, diverting your attention. This will lead you to recall memories of earlier times and places that will flood into your awareness, scattering you in many directions; your concentration will be lost. This happened because you deliberately listened, responded, accepted, and allowed the thoughts to continue. You are subservient to your conditioned beliefs. You lend support to these – assistance, and serve as one inferior of power. And have forgotten that I am your true power.

With love, from your inner self.

Knowledgeable yet unqualified!

Does a piece of paper qualify us as an expert?

Yes! We live in a world where credentials, titles and additional letters following a name is seen as impressive, that one is learned or has expertise. The influenced information has us believe that someone is a scholar, an expert or superior because they have completed their studies, studies that really are only memorisation.

There are experts that advise parents on raising children yet they are not parents themselves. There are experts that guide us in many areas be it health, relationships or wealth and they show little or no evidence of it in their own lives.

One may have perfect health, and they have achieved this through trial and error by establishing what in the natural world that surrounds us IS the recipe to truly attain this. However, they have no credentials to qualify them as an expert.

One may know all there is to know to live a full and happy life, understanding psychology and how the mind works, yet are they considered an expert, are they at liberty to share this with others on a mass scale, or must they attain credentials, printed on paper that gives permission to share this knowledge.

We are subservient to these beliefs. Beliefs that a title or printed paper means qualified. We assist in sharing them to others, advising our friends or loved ones of a service because the one offering a service has a title. A title they received through studies and memorisation.

We continue to serve beliefs, thinking credentials or a certification means wisdom, knowledge or expert, we even act on this conditioned thinking by wanting to gain a piece of printed paper ourselves. And this lends support in creating more invented titles.

What is an expert? from *expertus*, "tried, proved, known by experience.

An expert is only qualified when they have experienced it. A top surgeon becomes an expert only after numerous surgical procedures, through practice and repetition. A reformed drug addict becomes an expert in counselling other drug addicts because of their experience. It is the experience, not memorisation which evolves us to being equipped to receive the title of expert.

Life coaches are becoming more and more available. Where did the title, 'Life Coach' come from. Whose imagination first created it? And what qualified them to be the qualifier? What qualified anyone who invented an idea to be the qualifier? Did they have a piece of paper stating they were experts to teach this and hand out certificates? I don't know, do you?

Well, over twenty years ago I taught art and floristry at a technical college. I had no piece of paper, only the evidence of works showed my ability. This did not affect my students at all, each flourished in the lessons and created wonderful works. Quite a few years ago I began my studies in modern medicine. I achieved pieces of paper along the way and this governed how I was to help another get better. Health care professionals are to stay within protocols and be accountable to a medical body, an association who stipulates policies and procedures. These policies and procedures included commonplace methods and waiting plans that assisted in stretching out a condition. This did affect the patients and not all regained wellness, in some cases they became worse.

I mentioned a Life Coach earlier on. A Life Coach is a helpful person offering a service with intentions to aide another towards a better life, by guiding their client in taking responsibility of their actions. I became a life coach as well. I studied and received my printed piece of paper, however, this was not enough to make me feel like I had achieved my true desire. Our conditioned beliefs have taught us to look outside of our self for suggestions and answers. I chose to listen to the advice of others, who with good intentions believed certain career options to be best. And though I did not find my souls desire, I did achieve the beliefs, patterns and practices of the institutes I studied with, including the medical association.

The word life is from *leip,* "to remain, persevere, continue; stick, adhere". Coach is from *coche meaning* "large kind of carriage." As a certified Life Coach, I was now a *'persevere large kind of carriage'* with new conditioned beliefs and desires. I believed that many people across the globe needed help, and I was qualified to do this. What I did not know is that each and every person on this planet is just as helpful as I am. They are helpful to themselves!

Within each of us we contain all the answers; all that is required to achieve our desires. Sometimes these titles can make one feel inferior because they believe someone is smarter, more knowledgeable, an expert, and that something outside of themselves is the answer. It is not until we become aware, practice and learn to settle the clutter of conditioned beliefs that our soul voice can be heard. Here is where we find our own, unique answers that truly give us joy and abundance. And our life's purpose.

The best ideas come without effort. They can be the things we enjoy and do repeatedly or they can emerge into our conscious mind through unconditional thought, and when we add our 'why', this evokes us to think more of it, speak of it or write down these thoughts creating words or images that begin to take on a life form, our unique stories. Imagination is the beginning. Imagination is everything that we create in thought including both factual experiences and fictitious creations, if a concept does not yet exist in the physical world it will when we use the totality of mind, our imagination. And it is these thoughts that hold boundless and infinite potential for unfolding our life's purpose.

Let's take a look at some individuals that played with their imagination... authors. Jules Verne, Lyman Frank Baum, Enid Blyton, Jane Austen, Mark Twain, William Shakespeare, Virginia Woolf and Charles Dickens.

These authors have a common denominator. They wrote how they wanted it to be. They carried through their ideas regardless of customs, what was expected of them as a citizen and they were not subservient to conditioned beliefs. They replaced their patterned thinking with their own perceptions, they made choices to live their existing reality in their unique way and with passion. Shakespeare invented words, changed nouns into verbs, verbs into adjectives, and connected words never before used together. Jane Austen's novels were considered too daring both politically and socially for Victorian era expectations. People still bought them, read them, listened to her speaking of them and her works gained her historical importance among scholars. Through their passion, these authors shared their imagination leaving a legacy of written works to stand the test of time for generations of readers to enjoy. And they have showed us to follow our own path. They overcame their conditional thoughts and conditional beliefs.

What of non-literary Authors? All people who have, do and will exist in life are writers too. Everything we imagine is a blueprint of what is to become, whether we know it or not. The greatest story tellers are those who have attained success in their chosen path be it health, wealth, happiness or great relationships. They follow the path of unique greatness, they invent the new to suit themselves and harmonise with the unwavering law: The Law of Attraction. Like attracts like. Like thoughts attract like results. Your thoughts become things, your imagination creates your reality. And it is through the use of the Imagination that this Universal Law can be your blessed personal assistant or present to you negative unwanted experiences.

Be not subservient to conditioned thoughts or beliefs. Do not allow these conditioned thoughts to be attracted back to your reality. You are in control, be only subservient to your unique desires. There is no one, no title and no custom greater than you. You just as each person have a unique greatness that no other can match. You are an expert at something because you have a unique soul print.

Everyone has attained something great. Whether it be thought of an invention, a way to get their friends laughing, a clean and peaceful home or a handy hint that eases a chore. Everyone! Whatever we do, and regardless of how many times we repeat it, if we still enjoy it, this is passion, and our soul's voice is speaking to us. If an idea comes to mind without effort, our souls voice is speaking to us again. We can recognise this because it makes us feel good.

Carry and be inspired by your unique ideas regardless of what the masses do or what is expected of you just as Shakespeare and Jane Austen. Make choices to live your existing reality in your own way and with passion so that it may be archaic (from *arkhe,* "a new beginning for you; a time of merrymaking, amusement and festivity"). You will have much to celebrate because you WILL achieve your soul's desires when you say goodbye to your conditioned beliefs.

What is your unique experience? What makes you feel good and you could do it many times?

"The only thing that interferes with my learning is my education. And... The only source of knowledge is experience" – *Albert Einstein*

I am my own creation

Books! Books are a world of possibilities- containing words of leisure, emotional triggers, wisdom or simply present an escape from our routine life. Allowing us to pretend for some moments that in our minds we can live a dream; bringing an excitement, desire or comfort that uplifts us. They can help us to simply unwind; inspire us to greatness and growth; or even build upon our own inspiration. And most important of all; it is books, that are our highest tool to enhance and activate our imagination.

Books are also more than our teachers or an escape, they through evidential scientific research physiologically grow new neural pathways within the cells of our remarkable organ, the brain and this is achieved through our senses; we touch the texture of the pages and hear them when we turn to the next page, the scent enters our nasal passages and affect our taste buds, and we see the words, all of which sprout and grow neurological pathways from the dendrites.

The brain uses cells called neurons to generate and relay electrical messages to the body. Neurons are the *Manager* of the body, and they control the functions of every other system, communicating and coordinating performance from moment to moment. One of the most important components within the neuron is called the dendrite. For neurons to become active, they must receive stimulation. Dendrites are the *Managing Director* that control and receive electrical messages; and the stimulation for neurons to become active. When a neuron becomes active it has imprinted the information from the dendrite already determining how we will act, think, move, speak, taste, hear and the outcome of our entire physical body.

Dendrites can be likened to branches of a tree. This system of branches sprout, connect and grow in size, from information we receive in our environment. This information is absorbed through our senses; sight, sound, taste, touch and smell, and this information creates actual patterns, branching dendrites that develop in the brain.

These branches are energy channels where information or energy is stored and transmitted. Not only do we transmit to our physical environment, including our body, we transmit to the intangible, the invisible, the Universe, the formless substance, through our dendrites. It is our physical connection to our non-physical. We are a physiological transmitter! And the stronger and longer the dendrite the more powerful a transmitter we become.

Albert Einstein and Thomas Edison both explained; *the human brain is both a transmitter and a receiver of frequency. This frequency or energy is quantifiable and measurable and this energy exists in everything on the planet. It emits frequencies (just like a radio channel) which when focused are picked up by other human brains and/or matter through the ethers, these frequencies pass through solid objects, travels faster than the speed of light and can be picked up at the exact same moment by another human brain / mind / body aura on the other side of the planet, with exactly the same amount of energy. There is a magnetic pull, whatever frequency you emit, the same frequency will be drawn back to you.*

"The brain is a transmitter and receiver of frequency." We have the ability to create any frequency through the use of imagination. Whatever we choose to hold, practice and believe, the dendrites will welcome the frequency. Our senses are influenced by our external environments. The beliefs we hold, shared by the customs leave an imprint in our brain, branches of dendrites. The more we hear it, see it and believe it, repetition will

strengthen and grow the dendrites; and this will strengthen the transmission. Remember this...

YOU are a physiological TRANSMITTER. Whether by imagination, choice or conditioned thoughts and beliefs, you will achieve the results. What you want, wants you! At any moment you have the ability to choose what frequency your brain emits. Awareness of the frequency; conditioned thought or belief places you in a position to choose whether you desire the outcome or not, you have the power to accept, reject it or create something new. When we act on awareness and practice transmitting that which we desire we allow the universe to respond by delivering these to us.

How can we change our dendrites?

We can't. We can however create new patterns, grow newer stronger, longer ones! And we do this by:

Observing someone else: If there is a result we desire to experience in our life, and someone else has achieved it, we only need to observe and put into practice what this others conditioned thoughts and beliefs are (monkey see, monkey do). This is the reason for associating with someone who has what you want. It creates new neural pathways, new dendrites. Be mindful though, if we observe negative habits we begin to mimic and model them unconsciously. Observe carefully.

Read books: Books create new neural pathways faster than our eyes. Choose your books carefully though. To know this is to understand the statement; choose your words carefully. Choose what you read carefully for it will become a physical mark upon you and aid in creating your persona and physical experiences. Avoid reading anything that does not suit your desired outcome.

Write: Journal your thoughts, journal your desires. Writing by hand on paper is a powerful process. It is using the mind to think twice and to focus; focus declutters the mind, keeps one in the now, the present moment, and the junky concerns dissolve. To enhance your transmission write an endorsing list to yourself:

>Everything I like about my appearance.

>My personality is great because…

>I have strengths, what are they?

>I am proud of myself because…

Choose some people in your life and list: What you love most about them; their strengths, personality and appearance. If you can, reach out and share this with them.

Why? Because sharing positive emotions expand the dendrites too.

We are who we are right now and our experiences from past to present only exist because we repeated the practices and fed our thoughts by speaking of them, thinking them or believing them. These conditioned thoughts and beliefs installed into our minds only govern our experiences because of repetition. Ensure when you choose your new beliefs and practices that you repeat them over and over again, feed them often so that you create stronger, newer neural pathways that will overtake the old habits. It may sound simple, it is! However, many neglect this part. Distracted by their conditioned beliefs, beliefs that do not teach the all-important nature of repetition. Some know that repetition is imperative to bring to us new, desired experiences yet, they do not apply it. Stephen Covey stated this well, "To know and not to do is not to know."

Practice Makes Permanent!

Choice of illusion

The transition of building the rocking horse led me to reawaken my unlimited imagination, that wonderful flow of imagination we innocently enjoyed in younger days without the clouded thoughts of responsibilities and layers of other people's opinions (from *opinion,* "view, judgements founded upon probabilities"). My conditioned thoughts and beliefs, the mask of who I had become, the illusions of my beliefs began to dissolve.

What do I want? What do I really want to do? I asked myself this when the conditioned thoughts interrupted. My confidence was increasing. I had questions. Why is it not ok, what's so hard about doing it - others have, why is it a man's job; women have hands, minds and abilities? I could not see how gender determined what we could do.

Despite my thoughts and intuitive feelings of (there is more to life), I continued for many years avoiding giving a response to these intuitive feelings and took no action to find a solution to my thoughts. I accepted my seat on the evasive clone carousel without hesitation, ignoring my true feelings or own ideas, believing this to be the right and the adult thing to do- up until 1995. As the belief in myself evolved, I allowed my imagination to become a natural and acceptable part of my ways regardless of my earlier influences of how to act or think and most importantly I learned to relish these occasions with my head being in the clouds.

I began to understand that we can take a concept from our thoughts, evaluate it, choose our own interpretation and allow it to grow as we please. I activated my choice pattern and removed influence. This allowed me to accept that it's okay to choose what we want for ourselves. Only we ourselves truly know what makes us content and happy and if we feel this, we inspire those around us as well as.

As you now know conditioned thoughts and beliefs are simply a guide passed onto us from others that were taught through conditionings. Our circle of people raised us with good intention and some of these ideas are wunderfoll and insightful, however, ask yourself, if I had the chance to choose the path of information in my life what would my core beliefs be? When was the last time I did something for the very first time? When was the last time I thought unconditionally? What could I imagine? This takes us on the path to rediscovering our whole self- our own unique soul print.

What is choice?

From *ceosan* "to choose, taste, try."

To choose! However, did you really choose? Or is what you think, believe and experience a choice of illusion.

A Placebo effect, also called a placebo response, is a circumstance where a fake treatment is carried out. Substances such as sugar, distilled water or saline solution is given to a patient with a suggestion that the substance will help with their condition. The patient is unaware that it is a fake treatment and numerous tests have shown that the patient's condition improves simply because the patient has the belief and the expectation that it will be helpful.

Nocent is a word that has been in the English language since the 15th century. It means "harmful". It is from Latin *nocebo* meaning, "I will be harmful." This is in contrast to *placebo,* meaning "I shall please." The placebo is prescribed to a person for relief. A nocebo is prescribed to a person for belief.

Numerous studies have shown that a therapist's words have a great impact on the patient and the outcome. They can improve the patient's health or they can seed an opinion that creates an adverse experience. The therapist's words, affect both the patient's mind and body and produce physiological changes. This is called the nocebo effect.

The nocebo effect is not only limited to the field of medicine. Factors such as expectation, beliefs, trust and hope, play a role here. If there is trust or belief in another, the nocebo can take effect, particularly if we believe the person advising us is more knowledgeable or better than us. We all have been exposed to this effect throughout our lives. It could be through watching the news, someone we perceived as an authority or professional, such as teachers or people we care about. Words are very important. Verbal suggestions of either improvement or decline induces nocebo responses.

Nocebo is common conditioning, advertising is a prime example for using this effect and this has been played with in contextual cues such as; color, shape or sound. After repeated associations with any of these incentives we are conditioned through the nocebo effect.

Many more studies have shown that the nocebo effect is the tool used as preparation for suggestion. This is 'induced suggestion' wherein the thoughts, feelings, or behavior of an individual are guided by implanted thoughts.

This technique is often called hypnosis.

Years ago, I attended a show performed by hypnotist Martin St. James. I was with a group of friends, and when the show began volunteers were requested. At our table a hand went up. My friend was excited and wanted to have a go. I was glad. Someone I knew was going on stage, and this to me meant it wasn't a setup, because I believed these shows only chose so called audience volunteers that were paid members of the scam. The show began and I watched my friend act like a puppy, and within minutes the puppy was gone then she and other volunteers were prompted to go sit on the slippery chairs. These chairs were coarse fabric, nothing slippery about them. I watched and laughed as each person on the stage sat on these chairs and all slid off with every attempt. My friend returned to the table, unaware that she had acted like a puppy or that she had believed a chair to be slippery. She was a little sweaty and tired though.

In 1969, Martin St. James produced a TV series in Australia called Spellbound, where he hypnotized large numbers of people to dance like chickens and fall down in a heap. He has been recorded as having hypnotised more than 1.5 million people and sometimes up to 40 at a time. There are many other hypnotists and many examples of hypnotism, where people would be touched with an unlit match and a blister would form. One can be hypnotised to see snakes, to fear snakes, to sweat, shake and cry all the while the audience watching only see a person who is acting crazy. So, why does this person see snakes, why did my friend think she was a puppy, why did all the stage volunteers slip off fabric chairs, why do people act like chickens and why does one blister from an unlit match? Because to them it is <u>REAL</u>. Just as the conditioned beliefs to us are <u>real</u>. And through the lens of our hypnotic state, the induced suggestion, we only see the conditioned beliefs.

Induced suggestion occurs from many areas. Through our environment, people, media, music and contextual cues. It is a very powerful psychological tool and marketing and advertising is all about psychology. Ads, whether they are video, audio, magazines or billboards, are all designed to induce suggestion. Advertising and marketing are built on the foundations of induced suggestion and the nocebo effect. This is why we feel hungry if we see an ad for food, a child so desperately wants that particular toy or we worry about our health and money, because we don't have enough insurance. We buy and do things and wonder why we bought it or did it after a period of time because it did not really make us feel great or it was not as fantastic as we first believed. We are hypnotised all the time, another induced suggestion comes along and layers over the previous one, and this continues while we give it attention. We simply need to be aware of this.

Imagine... if you could influence others by using simple trigger words. Imagine you could do it in writing and when you speak. Well, over time, we have all been skilfully hypnotised to accept certain trigger words and this process started long before we spoke our first word. Because words, altered definitions and conditioned beliefs, were shared with us from the moment we were born.

When a word (remember words are frequency) is used consciously and correctly, it has persuasive power. I have already used two of them in the last paragraph. The following are three powerful and hypnotic words used in sales and marketing:

Imagine: As mentioned in an earlier chapter this word already has a conditioned belief installed. We do not see imagining as a real task. It's just a mind-game of fantasy. And this is a window of no resistance.

You: is a .... (space) for your name. The word 'you' has no hypnotic power, it is the name it represents- Your name, that has the power. Many email marketers start with your first name and include 'you' several times in the email. Advertising promotes it, for example; "for you, and your loved ones." Years before there was an advertisement used on billboards including hands outs such as; flyers and posters. This advertisement showed a picture of Uncle Sam pointing his finger and the word 'you' written on it. From that power of 'you' (... the space for your name) many enlisted for the army.

Because: John E Kennedy created "reason why" advertising. We have been conditioned to believe; we want to know the cause of something or why something is the way it is. This advertising gives a reason why (the because) a customer should have the product or service – why they cannot live, survive, or go without this product or service.

We believe that our conditioned beliefs are our own choices. They are only a choice of illusion. We have unique choice, the power to notice and truly feel what is right for our unique self. Awareness directs us in making an unconditional choice. We can change anything, even induced suggestion in any given moment and we do this with awareness and unconditional thought.

Thought is: purpose or intention. A process of thinking by deliberation.

Choice is: to choose, taste and try.

Deliberately choose, taste or try 'different'.

It is through the power of unconditional choice that we can alter our conditioned beliefs. To start being and living in ways that truly make us and the people around us content and happy. It is not our responsibility to exist in a life that others want for us, nor continue to believe in outdated concepts that applied generations ago. Evolution has changed much of how we live and communicate, this is the way of our existence and evolution will continue.

A friend of mine was in high school over twenty years ago. When given a mathematical equation, such as; subtract 409878697 from 237657987986, he returned the correct answer within seconds, even within a fraction of a second! Whether it be subtraction, multiplication, division or addition, he did not use paper to establish the answer, he simply visualised it in his mind.

During high school in math class, there were tests where the formula in reaching the answer had to be shown and he did this. However, he had his own self-taught system and this often got him into trouble. The teachers showed him, on many occasions, the correct way to do math, the way we all should do it, yet, he continued solving math questions with his self-taught system. A system he disciplined, nurtured and believed worked. And regardless of how much he tried, he was unable to imitate the process shown by the educators. We are taught to add, subtract or calculate from back to front. He was opposite. In his mind he found the correct answer, every time, by starting from the front then going to the end. Teachers, including his parents saw this as defiant, and that he must respect what the professionals are showing, after all he is only young and adults know better.

His parents were not well educated and had experienced poverty in their upbringing. They moved from a European country to Australia well before my friend was born, they spoke broken English, and believed their lack of education as well as their poor beginnings made them inferior to the educated people. They felt these teachers were professionals and without a doubt, were best suited to advance their son.

The parents' meant no harm, they were concerned for their son's future and their intentions were good, yet, it was these intentions that dulled their sons' enthusiasm and the excitement he felt each time he had the correct answer. He took focus away from his genius and 'diminishing intent' took control.

The longer we wait to do something the less enthusiasm we have. Our wants are stored and sent to hibernate. This is the law of 'diminishing intent'.

When desires, inventions, hopes and dreams are acted upon and momentum is maintained it leads to succession of the goals. If an idea strikes we must make the decision to carry it through, action it in the time frame when our emotion is high, clear and powerful; when passion arises. Even if it is the smallest step such as writing it down or researching possibilities.

We need to be steadfast, not disciplined. The word disciplined is a common word used in the context of pushing oneself forward for self-improvement or self growth teachings. What we say to ourselves when we use this word is: I need to be; "physical punishment and to gain and learn; suffering; martyrdom," this is from *descepline.* When passion arises, you are 'steadfast', from *staðfastr,* "firm; faithful, staunch, and firm in one's mind."

Be steadfast, nurture your passion, maintain the idea, and feed the desire. You are a 'developer', from *desveloper,* one who can; "unwrap, unfurl, unveil; by bringing out the concealed possibilities." If we prolong an idea or do not act on our desires, the chances of success for our goal is reduced, our idea is overlapped with other influences and this idea begins to weaken. It falls deeper into the abyss of our cluttered mind, veiled by more influences in our growing years, and our passion suppressed to slumber alongside our hibernating goal. Our intent diminishes.

Back to my mathematical friend...

The circle of people in his environment did not observe the natural, pure and unconditional talent he expressed. He received no support in nurturing his genius, no direction to heighten the potential of his self-taught system, the desire was fading, and maintaining the idea grew into fear; he believed, this was being defiant! Because these adults only cared about his wellbeing. The belief in himself and the intent to one day be a scientific or mathematical pioneer diminished. His genius was sent to hibernate and still to this day he is dubious about reawakening it to its fullest capacity. However, now, it is not a matter of fear but that of regret. This regret grew to frustration and he has stewed on it for many years, he made a choice to numb his regrets with illicit sedatives and this has become his new master.

Imagine...

His desire and his self-taught invention was acted upon and momentum was maintained. Imagine he was steadfast and acted as a 'developer', bringing out the concealed possibilities within him, his unique soul print. Imagine, as the developer he unveiled the conditioned beliefs and knew all beliefs first began in one's imagination. Imagine he wasn't overlapped with other influences and his idea grew to a legacy… We could possibly have a mathematical system where no student struggles and is perceived as a dunce in math, a formula for engineering or a method for the greater good in science. The possibilities are endless and we can only imagine.

By the way, the word genius is from *genius,* "guardian deity or spirit which watches over each person from birth; spirit, incarnation; wit, talent." Also "prophetic skill and generative power." It is a root word from Gin "to begin, to beget." You, we, ALL have a genius within!

Whatever our individual choice, it is our responsibility to make it shine and to ensure we never allow anyone to dim our sparkle. To be our true self leaves no room for a list of negative emotions or conditioned beliefs and there is no effort in being yourself. There will never be anyone like you; yesterday, now, or tomorrow. Each of us truly are an individual and this is why finding this discovery, the discovery of our authentic, unique, unconditional and natural self is above anything else.

Recognise this...

Anything we give a definition to becomes a belief. This is attachment. Attachment is that which we give support to and this word is widely misunderstood. We have come to believe that uncluttering our physical environment is letting go of attachment. We carry out the task of clearing out cupboards, homes and breaking friendships that are labelled toxic. Regardless of how much we get rid of, be it our clothes, kitchenware, clutter in the garage, or even people, this will not bring the freedom we believe it will achieve. Ridding ourselves of things and people in the physical is only momentary, days, weeks or months. Then we revert back to feeling overwhelmed and dissatisfied. This is because we already have a sense of abundance deep within ourselves, reminding us of the 'Law of Supply'.

"You live in a universe of abundance. The universe will never run out of anything you desire and there is enough for everyone. It will always supply you with what you want, when you want it. You just have to ask." - The 30 Laws of Flow, Charlene Day

We cannot hear our soul's voice reminding us of our abundance, this is because the veil of conditioned thoughts is muffling it. However, we do have an instinctive and intuitive knowing and this is what moves us forward to accumulating more things as we go through life. We forget many of the physical things we have experienced before. Do you remember everything you have owned over the years, including all the items in the kitchen cupboards, your clothes, what they looked like and how many? Do you remember everyone you have met, spoke with and what they looked like? Your unique self will have already disregarded much of these accumulated experiences, only your conditioned thoughts will remember some, because those things are tied to an emotion. All that matters is that attachment has no relation to physical things or people. It is attachment to conditioned beliefs that stands in the way of our freedom.

The Law of Detachment states:

In order to successfully attract something, you must be detached to the outcome. If you are attached, you project negative emotions of fear, doubt, or craving which actually attracts the opposite of your desire. You are operating from a position of worry, fear and doubt rather than serenity, trust and faith. Let go and let God.

This Law at no point states let go of your physical belongings. It states 'you must be detached to the outcome'. We control our attachment to conditioned beliefs and we have chosen fear, doubt, cravings, or concerns to be real; and made them part of our life experience. When we detach ourselves from these beliefs (beliefs that were originally created from another's imagination) we are free without concern for the outcome, because we intuitively know we live in a Universe of abundance and there will always be a supply for what each of us desires, including the opportunity to promote our genius. The Universe is here to serve us as we serve it, we work in harmony and our wonderful Universe gives to us everything we ask for, every time. Including our conditioned beliefs.

Deepak Chopra wrote: *"Embrace the unknown and watch how creative solutions to problems spontaneously emerge. Realize that the more uncertain things seem to be, the more secure you will feel, because uncertainty is the path to freedom. Step into the field of all possibilities by staying open to an infinity of choices. As you flow through your asanas (posture in which he or she sits), you can also practice the mantra that resonates with the Law of Detachment, reminding you to release the need to control."*

Thank you, Deepak, we certainly do have a field of

all possibilities and it is time to dethrone the conditioned beliefs that govern how we are to experience life.

Say this aloud… "I have Dominion over my beliefs and have no need for attachments." Allow this to be your mantra. Or find other words that EMPOWER you.

Because you truly do have rule and power over your conditioned beliefs. You can remind yourself that you are a heretic- one who is "able to choose." At any given moment you can set boundaries such as; what you choose to believe, who you choose to listen to and how long for, what you will read, watch and hear and what you will not, and who or what you will be subservient to. These boundaries are foundations for your new outcomes in life.

When the weight of the conditioned mask is removed, this liberating, unconditional self brings with it the positive flow to others. As opposed to conforming (from *conformer,* "to make or be similar, be agreeable") to the trap of conditioned beliefs, which takes the opportunity of your passionate legacy away from others and the inspiration intended to be shared with future generations irretrievably lost.

"The opposite of courage in our society is not cowardice…it is conformity." —*Rollo May*

It is when questions of our beliefs are probed carefully we discover that we have done the same thing over and over again, similar to our previous generations or ancestors. We reap what we sow and we are sowing other people's ideas.

"Don't compare yourself with anyone in this world...if you do so, you are insulting yourself." — *Bill Gates*

"A human being is a single being. Unique and unrepeatable" — *Eileen Caddy*

"There is just one life for each of us: our own"
— *Euripides*

Part III
YOU! Are the Creator

Three wishes granted

Dear inner self,

"How can I think myself as a unique energy signature?" My reply, "I do not know. This question has wrapped me in darkness, that cloud of unknowing. It is possible for me to have extensive knowledge of many subjects, even history. I have no difficulty in thinking about such things, but I find myself incapable of thinking of my true self with my inadequate mind, a mind tainted with conditioned beliefs. Enough! Enough, I say, of this torment and confusion. Let me abandon everything within the scope of my thoughts and determine to love what is beyond comprehension and have the courage to step above such ideas with devotion. I pierce that thick cloud of unknowing with a sharp arrow of longing love. I surrender, I admit, I am superior, not the shadow of another. I am because of you, I am you and you have patiently waited. I will not turn away no matter what happens."

With love from your creation, physical self.

Imagination is: Unconditioned thought and an unconditional mind. Think back to when you were a child, unfettered by conditioned limitations. You are about to be given three wishes that will come true. What will you wish for?

However, before you begin your wishes there needs to be awareness and understanding first.

Let's begin with the word co-creator. What does this mean?

Someone who creates jointly with another.

You! Are a co-creator. You are a segment of the Divine Creator: God, Universe, Source or whatever word or title you choose to call the power of creation, the ALL. The word has no relevance to what or who you truly are. You were given the gift of independent nature and consciousness (awareness). This is why there is and will always be that inner feeling of something bigger than the physical identity. *"I say me, knowing all the while it's not me."- Samuel Beckett.*

You ARE already excellent. Nothing needs to be fixed or improved. The totality of who and what you are already gives you all the tools to create by choice. You are simply being reminded.

The seed of you is the essence of the Creator. And the Creator is excellent. You and all people were granted the same ability as the Creator. This is what the bible refers to when it states *"God created man* (human being or person) *in his <u>own</u> image." (Genesis 1:27).* And... *Thus, He finished His work with a "personal touch. God formed man from the dust and gave him life by sharing His own breath." (Genesis 2:7).*

"Go forth and create worlds without end in my name."

'Creating worlds' meaning to create physical events, objects, sensations and emotions. 'In my name' means your independent nature and you as a Co-Creator, one who creates without doubt, is infinite, absolute and without limitations, just as the Divine Creator. The core of you IS the Divine Creator and the Genie of your own experiences. You carry with you all the abilities to create as you go, at any given moment and the free will to choose how you wish it to play out. You have the limitless power of imagination. When you imagine you connect to your unconditional, limitless and continuous capacity. It's already in the word;

Imagine

<u>I'm-a-gin-e</u>

I'm a begetter

You are the one who begins the transmission to the formless substance. You are the one who creates your life outcomes.

Your wish, as and when you command.

We are always given what we want whether it is conscious choice with deliberate concentration or by default through the conditioned thoughts we believe to be true that exists within our mind.

From the time you showed up as a cell in this physical existence you have been experimenting, striving, learning, succeeding and failing at times. Your learning taught you that everything is happening to you, however, this is far from truth. Your world, your experience is happening <u>for</u> you. It responds to everything you hold in your patterned thoughts accumulated through the environments you have been exposed to. Environments include everything you have cultivated and practiced through the sensory system of sight, hearing, taste, smell and touch.

We are the Co-Creators of our every moment. Before this life journey began we had already chosen which conditioned beliefs we wanted to begin with. When we were born into this physical existence, our experiences, the parents and environment are of our own choice. We knew we would be implanted with specific beliefs in our earlier years. Louise Hay in her book, *You Can Heal Your Life* wrote *"Each one of us decides to incarnate upon this planet at a particular point in time and space. We have chosen to come here to learn a particular lesson that will advance us upon our spiritual, evolutionary pathway. We choose our sex, our colour, our country, and then we look around for the particular set of parents who will mirror the pattern we are bringing in to work on in this lifetime."*

We chose it and it is our work to listen to our soul's voice to evolve from the initial chosen experiences. Without these fundamental experiences we cannot evolve into the ultimate purpose for the visit of this lifetime.

This lifetime is much like a holiday. We plan the holiday for specific purposes and to achieve certain results. It can be to physically see something, to learn of a new culture by immersing ourselves in that culture, to taste things, to feel things or to simply relax and absorb the scents, sensations and seascape of the holiday destination. We also have unexpected surprises, unplanned experiences or difficulties. It all depends on how we choose to view the difficulties, through our conditioned beliefs or our unlimited imagination.

Through our life structures and patterned beliefs, we have already disregarded possibilities, most of the time without awareness, and this is an interruption to our evolutionary pathway, our ultimate purpose. We carry with us sync sabotage and our focus is diverted to whatever thought we give dominion to.

Sync sabotage is high vibration emotion; feeling good or happy merged to a circumstance of a lower vibration emotion; sad, fear or shame.

At one point we have had an experience where we were feeling good and something happened that did not feel great. For example; when were children, we may have been playing having so much fun, feeling free and got dirty, then our parent berated us or perhaps smacked us for messing up our clothes. And whilst this berating or smacking occurred our minds were still in the processing phase of feeling good, free and fun; and when naughty, pain, fear or shame appeared during the processing phase of the mind it merged, creating sync sabotage.

Another example is that we had a pet, toy or person we loved that was taken away from us. In the moment the pet, toy or person was removed, including deceased, we still felt the love and were in the phase of love. Our mind registered love and removed or deceased, merging them as one, and created a conditioned belief as well as a conditioned response.

With these events we experienced both negative and positive simultaneously. Our thoughts still carry the high vibration emotion and we add the negative moment, such as berating or taken away by focusing on it. Our minds go into a state of muffled vibration.

If we focus on the negative during the muffled moment of feel good/feel bad, this starts a process of amplification and forces us to separate our concentration from the feel good phase, and it accepts all the thoughts; that being berated, dirty, feeling free, happy and love <u>is bad</u>. We have created a blend of positive and negative as one, sync sabotage (something that disrupts, spoils, mismanages, and walks noisily in our thoughts). A process where when something in our future actually feels good the saboteur, the conditioned response, will surface in our thoughts.

These new conditioned thoughts and responses have created a mechanism of distraction, therefore, whenever something occurs that can be related back to the moment sync sabotage was created, disruptions and noisy thoughts emerge, for example; when we meet someone and fall in love, love has synced with 'bad'. Sync sabotage has blended 'feel good' love with love gets taken away or becomes deceased. The distraction mechanism will kick in because we are experiencing the 'feel good' love and we automatically sabotage the relationship with beliefs of bad and that it will not last because it will be taken away from us.

We exist in duality, from *dualis*,"two". Duality is the Law of Polarity: everything has an opposite; up or down, hot or cold, happy or sad, love or indifference, asleep or awake. And opposites exist simultaneously, at the same time. Duality such as yin and yang must exist for balance. Every moment IS yin and yang, positive or negative. It is what we give power to, dominion over and what we place our focus upon that wins the moment. When sync sabotage arises, recognise it and don't give the power to it, don't believe it. Question yourself. Is there really something to be unhappy about? Why feel bad if there is so much to be happy about? Is love really bad or your partner not worthy of your love? Find many questions that will weaken the belief.

We have duality on our side. Let this be your friend and 'LIVE ON PURPOSE'. Purposely choose what you <u>want</u> the outcome to be. Disregard the part that feels bad and distract your focus from that onto the part that makes you feel good, even if it is to shrug the shoulders, take a deep breath and start humming a tune. You CAN divert your focus to a new vibration and feel good any time.

Another way of overcoming sync sabotage is to simply realise that it is okay not to be 'perfect'. Surrender any need for perfection, this cannot exist because energy is always vibrating, moving, changing, expanding and flowing from moment to moment. Perfection can never be. Surrendering perfection leaves no room for justifications and excuses; more mental chatter to clutter our mind. When we surrender we accept a state or experience as 'it just IS', and this peaceful moment of no resistance gives back power to us so that we may choose our response without yielding to stresses of sync sabotage. We can either let sync sabotage overwhelm us and trigger us into creating a fictitious justification for an outcome or we can use sync sabotage to our advantage for more recognitions of conditioned habits. Sync Sabotage or in fact any 'feel bad' experiences, is a signal pointing out something we need to reject. This is a way we can read our conditioned thoughts and reflect on what it is we carry within the mind. It is an opportunity to take our power of control back. Remember we exist in duality, we at all times have two opposing thoughts. Choose a thought that suits your desired outcome and start performing the way you want to believe and your mind will change to match your performance.

Another guide to bear in mind is the Law of Relativity: Everything just 'IS' until we compare it to something. Nothing is good or bad, big or small, unless we measure it with something else. Nothing has any meaning, except for the meaning and judgement we give to it.

To truly look out through the lens that shows the outside experience is to see that everything is simply composed by us and we are incredible manufacturers of the term we call life. The outside world reflects our inside world and this is marvelous when we observe what we have created. Good or bad, we have the power to have created it. We really are fortunate to have many experiences and demonstrations reflecting the power of us. Success is having gratitude for our ability, being in the present moment and feeling the experiences we have brought to fruition. Even if we perceive them to be mistakes.

There are NO mistakes. Our conditioned beliefs tell us that a mistake is a negative action and failure…BAD! Some say it is a great process in learning and moves us forward to our desired goal. This is getting pretty close to the true meaning. What is a mistake? It is "take in error; miscarry."

Mis-take is to mis-carry.

Thoughts taken because beliefs are carried. You have the choice to take and carry new thoughts anytime. Remember YOU are a Creator.

A Creator doesn't make mistakes; a Creator just creates! And creates a diversity of things, in many different ways. If we are not experiencing our desired result, we have only mis-taken and strayed off the intended path. When Tomas Edison created the light globe, there were many attempts before he attained the result. He did not make mistakes, as he stated, *"I have not failed. I've just found 10,000 ways that won't work."*

In these 10,000 ways what he also did was create 10,000 other ideas. Ideas showing ways in doing something else and ideas that can come to fruition for many other inventions. Mistake is our friend that guides us to doing more things and having more experiences. It is our gift that triggers us in trying different things, things that can be expanded upon in the imagination. And the 10,000 mistakes we have created in life, lay waiting for us to write a book, compose a song, share a story of hope when speaking with others or invent a product to ease one's way.

Have you jointly worked with another, have you spoken with another, sharing thoughts, ideas, ideas you may expand, perhaps sketch a draft on paper to further explain your concept? If so, it's time to do it with yourself. You are and always have been at work within an infinite power. Work with yourself, speak with yourself, draft ideas with yourself, sketch them, write them, and choose your new desired experiences…Play with possibilities, even how you can improve or change a mis-take, by using your imagination.

Up to now you have steadily made progress by a vast array of experiences and now is your opportunity to become a participant in the creation of new self-chosen experiences regardless of perception. There is no right or wrong, only what would you like to experience next. You and only you know what feels good or not so great for yourself. You did this as a child, the world was full of opportunities. You never grew up, the essence of you cannot age. You simply evolved, evolved with other people's opinions. Pick you own and enjoy the process of your own creation.

Be aware of your emotions and your thought patterns, whether by design or automatic conditioning. It will determine the quality of the vibrational patterns. The emotion frequencies are the seed thoughts you plant in your personal creations and will determine the quality of what you will bring to fruition in your experience. Emotions are much like a GPS. And the GPS is our souls voice. If you have steered off the route the voice of the GPS will say do a U turn. Our emotions, our souls voice is indicating our U turn to disconnect from the beliefs and to change the direction of our thoughts. If the situation does not feel good to you, don't surrender by feeding the emotion, move it along and change the frequency. Get up and walk about, shake your body, put on some music or if you can, change your thoughts to a better outcome. Whichever way you choose to move the frequency, it will change the energetic vibration of that moment. You are in control, not your conditioned thoughts.

Just because a conditioned belief exists within a thought it does not make it real. Be mindful that you live in a world of vibrating energy. A thought or belief is just vibrating energy and creation waiting for you to mold it into anything you can imagine. You create your own Heaven or hell. Beliefs are and always will be only words, an opinion and usually someone else's opinion. An opinion to be believed or disregarded as you go, choose.

Death and life are in the power of the tongue, and those who love it will eat its fruits. *(Proverbs 18:21)*

If you hold a thought to be true and you speak, sharing these beliefs to yourself or others, you love it. The formless substance will see this as your desire. Death and life, positive or negative, whichever you chose will become the fruits of your life results.

Createa new energy, a new conditioned belief, ones you love, not words of hardships. Choose beliefs that will fill your life with fruits you enjoy. After all you are the only creator in your experience, there is nobody that can do this for you unless you choose to embed and believe another's opinion. Have faith and love in all things. All things are creation, all things are nature, and it all comes from the same Universal source.

Recognise that you are creating your experiences right now, every moment, every day. It's your own personal novel and you can write a more satisfying one if you choose. You are in control. We view the internet as a fast way of connecting to our needs or desires, but the fact is our thoughts are greatly quicker than any internet service, regardless of advanced technology. Our transmissions, good or bad, will always be our intentions, but unlike our desires we obtain or purchase from the internet there will never be freight charges, only free delivery. Our intentions will always be delivered, however, the receive time will always depend upon the focus we place on our orders to the formless substance.

Get clarity on what you want and find your 'why'. Your why targets your mind to focus on your next creation, set a definite intention without resistance and it will assist you in noticing all the information, people and opportunities that can help you achieve your goals.

Prime your mind often, every day to create new beliefs and new habits. Speak with yourself, sing your result, talk to others about it, listen to audios that confirm it, write it, draw it, play act or just simply look at yourself in the mirror each day and affirm to yourself that you the creator of your life, your imagination takes you to what is right for you. And know that you are truly great. A giant of possibilities.

You have the tools of creation at your fingertips, release all that no longer serves you. You are a co-creator with the ALL. You are the Genie who can grant into your experience unlimited wishes, start with three wishes, and synchronise to these goals. To synchronise means to occur at the same time, in unison, followed with to recur: to return and do it again. Write them down, sketch them, feel them, smell them and smile with them. Use your senses as you write and sketch to synchronise them in the now. Explore new possibilities and choices and continually expand your vision of what is possible. Take action on them, even speaking of them, studying them or writing them down is taking action. Work with yourself, trust in yourself, follow what makes you feel good at any given moment and you will bloom to be a mindful co-creator leaving the default or conditioned creator as an experience in history.

The Law Of Relativity guides us: "Nothing is either good or bad, but your thinking makes it so." - *William Shakespeare.*

"An artist, under pain of oblivion, must have confidence in himself, and listen only to his real master: Nature."- *Renoir*

Cause of life

Cause: from *causa*, "reason for action, grounds for action; motive."

"A man sooner or later discovers that he is the master-gardener of his soul, the director of his life." - *James Allen*

"He who asks a question is a fool for five minutes; he who does not ask a question remains a fool forever." - *Chinese Proverb*

Questions are our tool. Raising questions help us expand, creates new possibilities, gives us the opportunity to assess problems from a new energy angle and we progress forward to greater experiences.

An energy angle, also known as Gods energy angle, is when energy becomes specific - specific meaning the angle is a unique frequency, a bar code so to speak. For example: We each became a physical existence at a certain angle, a specific moment at birth, a unique frequency. This angle is time and space. Time is the date we were born.

Space is the circumstances of our environment, who we are born to and where we enter into existence such as a hospital in London, England.

Everything physical and non-physical was created at a time and space; and has its own unique energy angle, including questions. When we choose a question we bring into our experience the frequency of new possibilities, and an energy angle that is already created. We all have an inner sense, an intuitive feeling of something greater and therefore we all fundamentally have similar questions. Many questions have already been thought of in a time and space and exist with their unique frequency. The unique frequency of a question enters our experience and the more we practice with this frequency we get the results of the energy angle created for the answers. Here's another example.

Each unique frequency is like a bar code used on a label of a supermarket product. When a product is scanned on the electronic reader it registers and knows exactly what the product is and its details. A question is a product, you mind is the scanner, and the formless substance is the register. Each time you scan the product (a question) in your mind, you register that frequency, and the formless substance delivers the details of this product, the answer. The more you persist by asking again and again, you surpass cluttered thoughts, including conditioned beliefs, because you are layering over them with new frequencies. This gives you opportunity to assess your present outcomes with the latest frequencies and you can expand these thoughts because you now have clarity to hear the answer.

However, it is how we choose to ask the questions that brings to us the energy angle results.

In an earlier chapter I mentioned how people were giving me clues as to why things were working out for me; "How do you do it? You're so lucky! You have an incredible imagination! I believed lady luck was on my side.

I thought to myself. Was I just 'lucky?'

I questioned myself, who am I to be so lucky?

I received no answers. I accepted not knowing and besides these were more rhetorical questions, a statement rather than something I deeply wanted an answer to.

I observed the people around me, I listened to their hardships, their ailments, financial woes and the array of stories they heard when watching the news, reading the newspaper or something passed onto them from another. I showed concern for the people, the information and cared about the burdens of the world. However, my experiences were different. My daughter and I were happy, healthy and my bank balance was comfortable. It did not feel pleasant knowing that my friends and others in the world were suffering. I thought, where is the fairness and the sense in it?

I asked myself more questions:

Am I just lucky?

Why can't they be happy like me?

What is the meaning of life, when people have to suffer?

This time something stirred inside me. I wanted to know the answers! I WANTED to KNOW! I craved the answers. <u>I believed there were answers</u>. And my thoughts kept on asking more.

We all reach a point in life and begin to ask similar questions, only the context can differ, for example: Why am I sick? Why is she so lucky? Or what do I want? There are many questions. And when we are unable to find the answers we turn to others, including books, anticipating the answers to be here, and these answers will settle the yearning, pain or noise in our thoughts. We only seek answers when we have reached a point of need, a point where we conditionally believe them to be our ticket to a better life experience, be it better health, increased wealth or lasting relationships.

Regardless of who or what we turn to for answers, we ask in vain.

Vain: from *vain, vein* "worthless, void, invalid, feeble; conceited, devoid of real value, idle, unprofitable."

Yet, to ask in vain along with our yearning to know IS the journey we must take in order to reach the ultimate destination, the meaning of life. And if not for this journey we would not reach for this answer. Because all the questions are answered in vain and they only give momentary satisfaction. We can be satisfied for minutes, hours, weeks or months and still feel a deep sense of 'there is still something else'. This is because our souls voice already knows the only answer.

There is no single answer to all the questions of life. No one has all the answers and no one has YOUR answer. We all are playing in an abstract experience. (*abstractus* "drawn away, divert; a smaller quantity containing the virtue or power of a greater.") Life is a drawn away experience, a change for our true self, our soul self and a playground of possibilities, possibilities we could not experience without physical senses. This is a game of life, and we, the <u>Soul</u> Creator - the Supreme beings who are primarily mind and matter are the players and we create through our imagination as we go. Just as you would cook spaghetti one evening for dinner, it was created for that moment 'dinner' and nothing more. Life has no meaning, it is a subject of our inner state, the Creator. And a creator simply creates, whenever and however we choose the physical to be, by design or by automatic conditioning.

The cause, motive, action and reason for life is… To live on purpose, purposely choose an intention for the aim or goal you <u>want</u> and then play in the field of your imagination.

And the key is for you to give life meaning. To deliberately bring meaning to it yourself. Your choice of meaning and not conditioned or conditional meaning.

Deliberately:

From *deliberatus* "resolved upon, determined."

No one has the correct answer for the questions. They too are Creators and cannot create for us, unless we believe their answers and words. Then they have influenced our creative power and this is conditioned belief. Not one though can give the answer to what we truly require… What is your unique energy signature, your unique purpose? Nor can they answer the question of what it is that truly makes one individual to another feel good. However, it is in asking questions, any questions, even if in vain, that begins us on the path to self-realisation.

"The one who asks questions doesn't lose his way."
– African Proverb

The questions we ask in vain are our catalyst, the dissolver of our conditionings and begin to guide us on the journey back home, to our unconditional minds. The desire I had was to bring to fruition a rocking horse for my daughter, and this was my trigger for the catalyst. Many conditioned beliefs flooded my thoughts and I had questions, many questions about these beliefs. Our questions dissolve beliefs, our questions recognise how useless and nonsensical they are.

When we override our conditioned beliefs and replace them with new ones, we also clear the clutter of 'feel bad emotions' and transform them into 'feel good.' We are then back in the flow of our true self, true self only 'feels good.' This will free us to hear our souls voice; and discover what we each desired to begin with, what kind of experiences and lessons we put on the itinerary before we came on this holiday destination, called the game of life.

Get ready to ask yourself questions, because all along you have waited to answer them. And remember, life is not purely about your unique energy signature, this is just part of your itinerary that you have chosen to experience prior to arriving in this physical body. You are here to see the views, test and try any physical experience you wish. You are the educator of yourself and imagination is there to expand your opportunities. And you can deliberately express whatever 'yours' is; experience, desire, feeling or belief. You are the seed of the Creator, just as the apple tree, and you can produce as many apples, branches, leaves, seeds and offshoots as you choose. Anytime, every time and all the time.

"Ultimately, man should not ask what the meaning of his life is, but rather must recognize that it is he who is asked. In a word, each man is questioned by life; and he can only answer to life by answering for his own life. To life he can only respond by being responsible."- Austrian neurologist and psychiatrist Viktor Frankl, once prisoner in Auschwitz, the Nazi concentration camp during the Second World War.

Beacon Body

"There is a way that nature speaks, that land speaks. Most of the time we are simply not patient enough, quiet enough, to pay attention to the story." - *Linda Hogan*

We were so thorough in planning and preparation to come on the journey of life that we packed in our minds a beacon body. Beacons of signs, signals and signal horns. Much like a lighthouse is the watchtower for the seafarers, which guides and informs of risk, our beacons are the watchtower for our physical, emotional, and mental bodies.

"It's not about learning to trust. It's about learning what it is I place my trust in and why. It's like learning to see the forest for the trees. You cannot see the forest for the trees unless you are outside the forest." – *Bashar*

Trust in inspiration! Not only in your environment and imagination but in what you already do - to inspire; inspiration also means to blow into or breathe upon.

"With each instant that I breathe, I feel the joy that life can bring"- Anonymous

Remember to breathe. The breath is the conductor of life force energy. Breathing through the nose and out through the mouth allows us to calm, and alters the vibration, raising vibrational frequency. The higher the frequency, the more unloaded we feel in our physical, emotional, and mental bodies. We unblock, release and unclutter our bodies; and create greater clarity for unencumbered power to return. Uninterrupted energy flow. As Bashar stated in his quote: *"You cannot see the forest for the trees unless you are outside the forest."* We need to be outside the forest, the clutter and blocks to be in a position to know, see and choose what our unique self wants, without conditional views impeding us.

Our physical bodies are secondary to our energy body. Any disruption in the flow of this energy pattern results in deterioration and dis-ease to the physical body. It is our mental state which governs the frequency such as; happy or sad, confused or peaceful, because we accept these as beliefs. And our emotional state, our beacon, our lighthouse, will signal us of our mental state, our thoughts, and guide us to keep going because we are on our way to abundance and our soul identity; or our beacon will blow a horn informing us of the risk, such as a headache, discomfort, sadness or anger, alerting us to divert our thinking to something else.

Emotions along with thoughts, solid objects, people, animals, plants and everything else in our Universe is made up of matter (energy, substance or content). Or as Wallace Wattles wrote in his book, *'The Science of Getting Rich'*- "*A thinking stuff that forms all things.*"

All physical and non-physical matter is composed of vibration, the same energy that resides within us. This vibrational frequency is different in everything, the frequency is determined by the number of components, such as; amount of atoms, molecules, protons, neurons, or electrons. There are boundless combinations and each vary, no two are identical and each are the results in the physical and non-physical realms. For example, no two leaves, people, flowers, cups, animals or chairs are the same in matter, each has its own unique energetic frequency that support their particular existence.

The Law of Vibration states: Everything in the universe is energy. It is ever moving, vibrating at different frequencies, and always shifting into various forms. These vibrations vary. Each of us are energy vibrating at a specific frequency.

Our minds are a vibrating force and every thought, including beliefs, is matter, vibrating at a specific frequency. Whatever frequency we hold we will match *"the thinking stuff that forms all things,"* and bring it into our physical experience. We are a 'thinking Creator'.

What is labelled as positive emotions such as love, happy, calm, joy or serenity is correlated to high or fast moving vibrational frequency. This is because these frequencies show signs of wellness, vibrancy, vitality and all that gives to us 'feel good' experiences. Lower or slower vibrational frequencies are what brings to us negative emotional states such as illness, depression, anger or lack of vitality.

In the previous paragraph I began with 'What is labelled.' This is because it is not the word, nor is it an emotion. We give emotions titles so that we may recognise them and this serves as another tool in our creating. Each emotion is purely a unique vibration and the frequency pattern or the composition of its matter gives us the unique sensation. The sensation of the frequency. The words only correspond when the words are used as they were originally intended.

The energy matrix of any experience is reliant upon

a certain frequency of vibration. It cannot exist if it has no frequency and we cannot have an experience without matching the thought to the frequency. When we alter our vibrational frequency, we directly affect our physical world. Therefore, if there are unwanted experiences, events, thoughts, sensations, or conditioned beliefs we only just need change our thoughts.

Back to our breath. Our breath is the way we connect the mental state with the physical body, it is also another tool in understanding our emotional thoughts (sensations) at any moment. Thoughts and sensations affect our breathing patterns and these patterns are indicators for controlling our experience. A calm breath is our indication of high vibration, of being in a peaceful state. Heavier, quick breaths indicate unease and this will create our unwanted experiences including ill health.

Breath is not only our conductor of life force energy; it is also a tool to reset frequency. Take a deep breath through your nose, hold it for a moment then release it from your mouth. Interrupt the frequency if you do not feel good and reclaim your power in any given moment. Let your breath be a reset and do this as many times as you require until you feel and hear the calmness of your breath.

"You seek too much information and not enough transformation." - *Sai Baba*

Transformation (change the form of) requires practice. A practise that is alien and conflicting to our conditioned habits. If it were not unusual and conflicting then we would already have transformed and have our desired outcomes, enjoying our physical creations. Our conditioned habits keep us in a dreamlike state, where we feel that a desired result is hard work or impossible to attain because of…….. You can fill the gap, if you choose. There is an array of excuses, from negative conditioned thoughts, and it is not worth the read. And it's just a bad, ridiculous dream.

If you don't like the dream you're in, wake up. Change the sheets and move the bed to another position. Transforming unwanted conditioned habits is no different to changing the sheets, and moving a bed. Awareness is to wake up, then recognise the conditioned patterns when they attempt to interfere with your new practises and at these moments you can dismiss the intruder who entered without permission. You are in control and give permission for entry into your experience, not your conditioned thoughts. We all must adopt a practise and change the form of our patterns to new conditioned patterns that are suitable and matching in frequency to our desired results.

When a frequency vibration accelerates it results to a higher vibrational frequency, higher feel good sensations and this can be achieved with ease. The faster we expand our mind with these high vibrational frequencies we place ourselves in more feel good sensations increasing our inner happiness and serenity. And this places us in a position to hear our soul's voice. Here are three ways we can do this:

The first is meditation! The word meditation is from *meditationem,* "a thinking over, reflect, consider." However, though this word is very much used as the term for going within, there is another term that is more suitable to this definition. Because, when we go within we free ourselves to; examine from within, look into, and observe our self and only our self, our soul self in the quiet of our mind, without the noise (sound and objects) of the outside world. This word is:

Introspection

From *introspicere,* "to look into, look at, examine, observe attentively, from *intro-* "inward".

We must have moments to calm our thoughts. We live in an active world of technology, attitudes, daily tasks, general living and conditioned thoughts. This is Self-

Knowledge practice and is <u>the most powerful</u> way to alter vibration and raise vibrational frequency. We enter introspection with movement of breath.

Going within or inward influences our physical, emotional, and mental bodies, rewarding us with wellness, tranquility, and an inner happiness that can only be experienced because words are not enough to describe the totality of this experience; and introspection invites more like frequency to keep flowing into our experience. It also amplifies clarity and this gives opportunity for us to have dominion over the conditioned thoughts and beliefs because the clutter dissolves. And introspection (meditation) is the place where you can hear the answer of your own heart, your soul's voice.

There are many ways to enter introspection. We can listen to a guided meditation, place soft, calming music on, or have a completely quiet space. You can use candles, oils or crystals if you wish. These, as well as calming music, all have unique frequencies and will add a successful result. We can sit, lay, head on pillow or not, there is no one way, only the way in which you feel comfort. Begin this practice with arms and legs unfolded, as folded limbs impedes the free flow of energy, and inhale through the nose, hold for a few seconds, then exhale out of your mouth, simply focus on the breath and this will begin the process of calm frequency. A helpful way to cancel out any distractions, from mind or external sounds is to count the seconds of breath. For example; inhale on the count of three, hold for two seconds and exhale on the count of five, releasing any unwanted frequencies held within your physical body. Just focus on your breath, wander deeper into a relaxed state and allow whatever enters the mind to flow naturally. There is no one way for this either; colours, one colour, faces, ideas or personal thoughts may enter the mind, it is your own unique experience.

Getting to know our unique self is the greatest occupation we can volunteer to our self. We can pursue and attain many things in life, believing an event or item will make us happy, however, when we receive these 'things' we are not as happy as we thought we would be, the novelty and excitement washes away within days, weeks or months and we are back to pursuing another yearning. How satisfied we are with the decisions we make is a measure of how well we know our true self. When we give our self quiet time to get in touch with our souls' voice and go within, we gain clarity and insight into what it is that we uniquely desire. These unique desires are the ones that give us bountiful happiness with lasting results. And the novelty will never wear off.

There are many things in life that are achieved through activity, however, our souls voice is one that comes to us when we stop activity, reflect upon our experiences, and connect to our unique self. We must give ourselves time to rest, recover and recharge. To go within is more refreshing than a deep night's sleep. It is a watchful and relaxed reset. A reset from the conditional thoughts to unconditional unique thoughts.

The second tool we can use to expand our mind to high vibrational frequencies is by music or sound. These each have a unique frequency to accelerate vibration:

Music: classical music such as Baroque enhances concentration. 528Hz tones and music, this is known as the miracle or love frequency and can be found on the internet. Soft calming music, such as natural sounds of water or birds also has high vibrational frequency.

Sound: audios containing music and speech of hypnosis and paraliminals. These are a process of induced suggestion. We have already experienced induced suggestions through repetition experienced from our environments, such as media, our families and school days, this is why we have conditioned beliefs. These audios induce new conditionings and we can choose the specific outcomes we desire. There are many to choose from here are some examples; health improvement, reverse aging, increase happiness, forgiveness, stop procrastination, intuition amplifiers or wealth mindset enhancement. These can be found on the internet as well.

The third vibration accelerator is Feng Shui. A science and ancient art based on laws for energy flow. This is practised through formulas and calculations using energy forces referred to as Qi (chi). Both Feng and Shui are associated with good health and prosperity. If energy in the environment remains stuck, people are prevented from moving forward, or may experience unwanted occurrences, however, by increasing the flow of energy this clears the path to propel us forward and to bring to fruition desired intentions. When changes are created in the environment it produces advancement and enhancement in the level and flow of Qi energy.

Our environment is our physical visualisation board and this unconsciously creates our outcomes, all day, every day. Just as everything is energy, our environment is energy and everything within it has its own unique vibration.

Feng Shui teaches that our external environment will always reflect our internal environment. When we shift or change our outer environment this becomes an energetic shifter to the inner self, the mind. If we align our physical environment with our desires this enables us to direct our lives, to change our experience and have command with how we choose our life experiences to be.

Look closely at your environment and observe what it is telling you. Can you see the reflection of your results? Can you see what is or is not happening in your life? Are there any objects or images that reflect a sad or angry life? Is there clutter? If there is clutter, this will add clutter to the mind.

Clutter management is a fundamental principle. Clutter fills our environment with too many unique frequencies, and can make us feel disorganised, uncreative, tired, anxious, overwhelmed and burdened. Think of clutter as not just a clutter of items, but rather as a clutter of energies.

It is essential for mental clarity and focus to create an environment, or simply a room with less furniture and fewer things that require tending to. When we have fewer distractions, we have stronger concentration and stay focused on our goals, it improves our motivation and energy flow. Look about, is there anything you can remove, donate or sell that will aide in calming your thoughts? Take action, clear out unwanted energy clutter and make room for more possibilities from your imagination. A Feng Shui consultant can be appointed for further assistance with improving your physical visualisation board. This service can be found on the internet or perhaps in your local area.

We are an incredible help to ourselves because we packed beacons for the journey of life, we have ways to accelerate vibration, we also gifted to our self navigational instincts. These are indicated by our mental faculties (capabilities of the mind). Our way to feel through and choose what truly feels goods for our personal experiences. These are;

Imagination: We HAVE (*habban*, "own, possess) unconditional and unlimited thought, always, anywhere, anytime and endless.

Choice: We CAN (*cunnan*, 'know, have power to, able, recognise, admit') choose between two or more unlimited possibilities and invent some through our imagination.

Intention: We CAN live on purpose and deliberately choose, aim or plan our desires.

Instinct: We HAVE stimulus in the mind that

produces a definite change of momentum. Unconditioned response. An urge that incites, rouses, encourages, and stimulates us to act.

Reasoning: We CAN question, argue and challenge. Just remember, to consider when reasoning, are you doing this from your unique self, or conditioned self.

Intuition: We HAVE the ability to understand something instinctively, without the need for reasoning. Our sensations, our beacons are our insight, direct or immediate cognition, and our spiritual perception.

Perception: We CAN interpret, regard or understand something. And recognise any 'something' how we choose to interpret or believe it, with or without influence and conditioned beliefs.

Memory: We HAVE a mind that stores and remembers information, cares, and thinks. We are not limited to conditioned thoughts only, within us resides the knowledge of the Universe and this is our true memory.

Creation: WE ARE THE CREATOR of our experience, and we are the triggers for thought to come into being, to create and produce a thing, sensation or experience.

Will: We CAN express a strong intention and

certainty; with no doubt and resolution. We CAN live on purpose for our desires. We request and command our outcomes. And we are fearless.

Fear is simply a clever ambush, an invention created in the imagination that declines our confidence and gives to us ill health and unwanted outcomes from the unique frequencies of anxiety and stress. Fear is an unpleasant stream of thoughts that are fuelled by conditioned beliefs. Beliefs of 'what ifs' and 'just in case'; the must do or not do something that lives in the future and not in our present moment. They are not real, and only become our outcomes if we willingly hand over our creative power to our conditioned thoughts that hold illusions of safety. Illusions shared to us by the media, news, family and environmental customs. Many of these beliefs were purely created to benefit the ones who created them, so that we may, buy, action or become the servant to someone or something. Do not view fear as bad though, this is simply another sensation from our beacon and it just 'IS'. The 'IS' has no meaning, it is fear-less and only becomes something when we attach a definition to it.

Of all the mental faculties intuition is the greater for Divine guidance. It is the inner voice, a hunch, a thought or sensation which says, "this is the way". A better description for intuition would be 'our spiritual faculty' that is above intellectual understanding. It is a magic path to our God within; our inner voice and sense that watches over us and never sleeps. Nothing is irrelevant with intuition because it guides us in the yay or nay of our next step. When we acknowledge our God within all our ways will be plain path for our unique greater good. Intuition has the power of eternal youth and eternal life because when follow our unique bliss we bring into our experience happiness and a physiology of ideal health.

We must be attentive to our God within and give lesser notice to reasoning and perception. Reasoning and perception can be tainted with our conditioned beliefs, and therefore not necessarily be our souls guide. Our intellectual understanding has taught us to reason through our conditioned beliefs, and sometimes it takes practice to notice only our intuition, rather than perception of circumstances; which is only habits. We have habits; regular habits that are accustomed to doing the same thing every day, such as; waking up and going to bed at a certain time. Any variation, in particular acting on our intuition, can upset our habitual behaviors, however, momentum in practice will overcome these habits that do not ultimately serve us. The practice of tuning into intuition is a must and an important part of spiritual development, because this is the straight line and shortest route to our confirmation of true self.

We began this physical life experience exposed to and educated by only conditioned beliefs. We had to start somewhere! From here, right now, we can learn from and gain insights from that which we do not want and change them into what we desire. We could never have known what we wanted had we not experienced the unwanted. Had we not had an array of experiences we would be clueless as to how it feels, because we have no comparison and we would not understand the Law of Polarity- Everything has its opposite, big or small, happy or sad, good or bad, positive or negative. It is our hardships that push us towards wanting to find a better way; we ask questions, find answers, answers that will eventually lead to our inner self. Remember, we did leave ourself tools; many beacons, ways to accelerate vibration, reset options and navigational instincts to guide us back home to our Soul Self.

"You have the Answer. Just get quiet enough to hear it." - *Pat Obuchowski*

"Who am I? is the only question worth asking and the only one never answered. It is your destiny to play an infinity of roles, but these roles are not yourself. The spirit is non-local, but it leaves behind a fingerprint, which we call a body. A wizard does not believe himself to be a local event dreaming of a larger world. A wizard is a world dreaming of local events." - *Deepak Chopra*

I give to you a magic pen

In this chapter you are to be gifted with a magic pen. But first let's get through some recognitions.

Our mind is the data bank of human consciousness and the vault is stored with every memory including; our unconditional thoughts and beliefs, all our hopes, all our desires, inventions that were dreamed, beliefs we had, and this gives us our true personalities, when we choose to unlock it.

Written works, be it fiction, or non-fiction, develops from the imagination. Life experience develops from the imagination. Every conditioned belief developed first from the imagination. And imagination is thought in production. Production and replication in the formless substance of the universe, to us known as matter. The thought becomes an idea, and an idea has definite potential of being life's coming attraction, a belief, a book, your story or your physical life experience! But, who's imagination is writing our experiences?

In our life experiences we are co-creating on two levels they are with our held thoughts and through our perception of the environment. This chapter is divided into both these levels.

Experiences of thought

I'll start this with a brief story, this excerpt from another book I have written titled, *Activate your Home or Office For Success and Money With Feng Shui.*

The two sat on the veranda, lounged on deck chairs, wiping the sweat from their necks and staring at the stillness before them. The day was too hot, where was everyone? Inside? The humming of air conditioners and the sound of a whimpering dog was all that could be heard.

The visitor sipped his ice filled lemonade and paused to look at the dog that lay less than a metre away, his eyes full of sadness and his head supported by both paws.

"Why is he whining?" he asked the host who was the owner of this dog.

"Because he is laying on a nail,' was the reply.

"Well, why doesn't he move?"

(This dog is obedient, subservient to his owner. Stuck with the belief that he cannot move his place or position until the owner allows it.)

The owner looked at his dog, sipped once from his own lemonade and replied,

"Because it doesn't hurt enough."

Whether it be our relationships, health, finances or personal growth, many do not change their situation even though it hurts us emotionally and is an unwanted experience. They wait until it hurts TOO much, before they take action to change their circumstances or their patterned thinking. Though these experiences come in different shapes and sizes there are similar patterns with many and we ask ourselves, why me? Why do I always pick the wrong person, why can't I feel better, why can't I be rich?

The questions to ask yourself are:

- Why wait until it hurts too much?
- What do I want?
- Why do I repeat the same patterns?
- What is success to me?
- What is wellness for me?

- What does personal growth mean to me?

- What kind of family, work and friendship relationships make me happy?

- What do I *really* want?

- How do I make this happen?

We live in a world where we have accepted statements and adages such as the rich get richer and the poor get poorer, it runs in my family, or, it's in my genes. Worse still we have held onto implanted beliefs of can't, hopeless, not worthy or unreachable. All these are purely opinions that have created lack and limitation in our experiences. However, all of these opinions began as a fictitious opinion through the imagination before they were created.

Remember, You! Are a co-creator. You are a segment of the Divine Creator and the core of you IS the Divine Creator and the Genie of your own experiences. Everything is possible and there is no lack or limit. Whatever exists can be created, including a whole new world of unknown possibilities, experiences and conditioned beliefs.

Any lack or limitation within any experience is only the outcome of the held beliefs. Beliefs of lack and limitation for health and money are common and are often present in people's experience.

We exist in a world where energy has taken form in physical transactions with an item called money. Your mind has already accepted this to be a belief and has created it as a tangible item that exists. This is neither good nor bad; evolution is a wonderful thing and we are all fortunate to be experiencing it in a variety of ways. However, if this is not a joyous experience for you then here's your moment to access your conditioned beliefs and see what you believe to be true. Write a list of how you see money, what does it mean to you, how much do you want, do you really need it, are some worthy of it and some not? This list will be your indicator to some patterned beliefs. Just writing them down begins the process of releasing unwanted thoughts.

What do you want? Is it good health?

The importance of wellness is imperative. Without good health many areas in our life do not function well, nor can we achieve our fullest potential. However, without necessities, comforts and money to buy good food, warm clothing, pay for the heating bill, or the services that can help with wellness, our health is compromised through worry or stress and we can even conflict with our loved ones. This amplifies poor health and the cycle returns again and again, giving to us a variety of ailments. Therefore, it is imperative to improve your financial wealth, more importantly our 'lack of wealth beliefs' to live life with a continuous flow of ease.

Wallace Wattles, *"The Science of Getting Rich"* wrote;

"There are three motives for which we live: We live for the body, we live for the mind, we live for the soul. No one of these is better or holier than the other; all are alike desirable, and no one of the three — body, mind, or soul — can live fully if either of the others is cut short of full life and expression.

A person cannot live fully in body without good food, comfortable clothing, and warm shelter, and without freedom from excessive toil. Rest and recreation are also necessary to his physical life.

One cannot live fully in mind without books and time to study them, without opportunity for travel and observation, or without intellectual companionship. To live fully in mind a person must have intellectual recreations, and must surround himself with all the objects of art and beauty he is capable of using and appreciating.

To live fully in soul, a person must have love, and love is denied fullest expression by poverty. A person's highest happiness is found in the bestowal of benefits on those he loves; love finds its most natural and spontaneous expression in giving. The individual who has nothing to give cannot fill his place as a spouse or parent, as a citizen, or as a human being. It is in the use of material things that a person finds full life for his body, develops his mind, and unfolds his soul. It is therefore of supreme importance to each individual to be rich."

To alter your experience with physical prosperity you must appreciate and accept the value in evolution. Accept money, technology and all the new creations with no judgement or limit.

There are many conditioned beliefs in regards to money that were shared with us throughout time such as money is the root of all evil. This statement has been much distorted. Money is not evil, nor is the cup you drink from or the clothes you wear, they are all simply items. It is how one chooses to use money that can make an event or circumstance unpleasant or wonderful. We all have a money story, the unconscious tale we continually tell ourselves about what money means to us, and what money says about us to others. These beliefs define how much we deserve, how much we think we are worth, and how much we are capable of earning. It's about what would happen if we had more and what would happen if we had less. However, we now know that our minds and the neural pathways (dendrites) can be changed. We are not stuck with the conditioned beliefs we were born with or beliefs accumulated up to now. Our mind continues to grow and change based on life experiences and the choices we make.

Know that each of us can have and deserve all the comforts we choose; this is why you chose to come into this life. You chose to begin with certain conditioned beliefs and to grow from there into your fullest potential. Experience what this lifetime has to offer and all the wonderful options we have before us. It is only a game, a game of life. Are you playing as yourself or is someone/s else playing on the game board for you? At any given moment you can begin to choose a thought of possibilities and practise adding to those thoughts with the knowledge that there are unlimited possibilities.

It is through our thoughts that we create, it is our imagination which believes and amplifies possibilities. Wallace Wattles in *The Science of Getting Rich* wrote;

"THOUGHT is the only power which can produce tangible riches from the Formless Substance.

The stuff from which all things are made is a substance which thinks, and a thought of form in this substance produces the form."

THOUGHT is the only power which can produce tangible riches - visible wealth found within - in personal relationships, finances and health. These thoughts may already live in the subconscious mind, your formless substance. Something, such as a notion or conception, can actually exist in the mind as a product of mental activity, waiting for years until the day an event, experience or a memory is activated, to release the flow of your imagination.

Or... through study, research and understanding we can create a force where our patterned conditioned thinking is replaced, allowing us to evolve, the formless substance expands and our perception of our existing reality changes. This enables us to divert our, interpretations, convictions and intentions to what we truly want. It is only when we have emotionally aligned ourselves and through the use of our imagination that we will produce the form of our thought and create it into our physical experience, every time.

If you have sensations that do not feel good or your thoughts are beginning to wander into unpleasantness, such as; lack of money or concern for ill health, get into the practice of distractor management. Start by preventing your concentration from remaining focused on the unpleasantness or in the negative. Divide the attention to something else, look out a window, walk around a furniture piece, hum, clap your hands or whatever you can summon up to change the vibration. Anytime you distract your attention, you will slip around your guard, your conditioned beliefs.

Remember this though. All realms of feeling and thought are given equal priority, there is no thing considered as good or bad. Even what is perceived as negative emotions can have its best moments. For example, when sadness occurs it is followed with new experiences, at any moment you can change this, yet, on some occasions just let it be, just observe them for what they are, just an experience and be grateful for the opportunity to feel what a tear is like upon the skin, or the strength of rage, or the anxious feeling that something is not right for you. They remind us of our navigational systems and beacons. These responses, reactions, and emotions are all part of you and creation. We are all duality; light and dark, good and bad, naughty and nice. They can be implemented within your control, used when a moment calls for it and never needs to amplify - you are in control. You can use any of these two; distract or observe, either way what only matters is your own personal choice, what makes YOU feel good.

Experiences of environment

Remember: Your environment is energy and contains many unique frequencies. This is your physical visualisation board, unconsciously creating your outcomes, twenty-four hours a day, seven days a week. I am about to give to you a magic pen to assist you in your environment, however, there is just a little more to add.

Every conditioned belief we accept to be true, rather than as just an opinion- ours or someone else's, unconsciously creates our experience. Within us resides shared beliefs that govern the outcome of our lives, such as our opinions of wealth, health, relationships or possibilities. Our environment collaborates as well because of our perceptions.

Everywhere we look, sit, stand, or listen contains information that encourages us to question ourselves as well as believe in structures and outcomes, such as the spiritual, financial, relationship, corporate and political experiences. There are varying layers of truth or untruth and all this is shared to us through technology, people and the written word. The internet, radio, television and all environments contribute to creating our conditioned beliefs.

We have developed beliefs where we look outside ourself for 'things' and ways to fill our void– 'outer hope'. We look to others for validation, authentication and acceptance of our worth. We think the physical world can provide us with security. We think and feel that we have to be more than what we are and get more than we have, and because of this we feel lack in ourselves and believe some of our present outcomes to be mediocre. This false belief of 'outer hope' has blinded us and feeds the hypnotic state that shrouds our immense capabilities. We reach out to others and bring them into our environment believing they are helpful, give good advice or know better. This is not to say there are no persons capable of truly guiding us. It is that we have not been conditioned to turn to the ones that can, instead we turn to, speak with, ask and listen to many others that have their own struggles and conditioned beliefs.

In addition, we observe signage, magazines, internet articles, audio and media advice; and any marketing, all the while increasing the clutter and beliefs of lack in our physical achievements and self because we need some 'things' if we are to get ahead or be better. Or so we are led to believe.

Your environment includes you, other people, structures, sounds, space, illness, wellness, hardship, emotions and 'things'; all environments play on any or all of your senses. This downloads the information straight into your formless substance and creates more conditioned beliefs, particularly the environments you visit often (repetition). Be mindful of this. Choose your environments to suit your desired outcomes. If the environment is displaying parts where you do not feel good... leave. If this is not an option, use tools to block out or override the experiences such as headphones or humming to yourself. At any point you have the choice to say this is not what I want and you now know that your thoughts will create your experiences. Never allow any unwanted outgoings to penetrate you in a way where you believe it to be true. Stand back and observe it as simply a moment in time. A moment that you choose to reject.

I give to you a magic pen.

You are being handed a magic pen as well as an everlasting pad of magic paper. Each time the paper is used a new one regenerates in its place. Every time you write or draw something on this paper it has your focus. Even before you have completed your ink creation it begins to actualise. Everything is pouring out in solid form and becomes a physical result. The pictures are obvious; they appear as the item you have drawn. Yet the words, regardless of whether they are an item, emotion, event or experience appear exactly as they are written shooting out a scene to match the frequency of the words. The physical results even impact you. You start laughing because it is funny, or you start crying because it is frustrating, or you tense up as you feel the anger unfolding.

What would you do if you had in your possession a magic pen and magic notepaper with an infinite number of pages?

Would you pick words that scare you, upset you or write words that entail impossibilities? Would you give it to someone else and let them write with it and on it? Knowing that this is your magic pen and paper. Only you get the results not them.

From conception, birth up till now and always, you already possess the magic pen and pad. Your thoughts are your magic pen and the length of time you hold these thoughts with emotion is your magic paper, the canvas of the

Universe. Everything you write with focus will become a physical result. You have let other people, other influences hold your pen for many years now, and it's time to take your pen back; and be in control of your outcomes. Write your own words, draw your own pictures, create your own conditioned beliefs, and keep applying your ink to your magic pad until the beliefs of the past are the ones that sink deep into the abyss of the mind; and the unused thoughts for unpleasant, unwanted outcomes, will be forgotten, and obliterated from your future. And... never again share or give your pen to another so they may flood your canvas with thoughts that do not make you feel good or does not serve your desired outcomes.

"Master of the universe but not of myself, I am the only rebel against my absolute power." - *Pierre Corneille*

"Experience is not what happens to you - it's how you interpret what happens to you."- *Aldous Huxley*

Misplaced memory

Mis- prefix meaning, "bad, wrong, divergent, astray."

Placed: from *placea,* "place, spot."

Can You Trust Your Memory?

Our memories shape our present mindset, and this plays a large role in our moment to moment decision making. Studies in neuroscience show that when a memory is formed in our memory storage, some of the details are disregarded during the upload process. Much like our physiology with food. Not all of what we eat is absorbed, we only take in a portion and the rest is discarded from our body's plumbing into the bathroom plumbing, the toilet. Unlike recording an event on our video camera, where we can watch the whole event including expressions and every detail in the environment, our memories archive only a summary of the experience rather than the whole, exact details, and this is based on our level of conditioned beliefs at the moment.

Every time we recall a memory, we tamper with it and our brains fabricate the missing pieces, the pieces that went down the plumbing pipes and we fill in the gaps with any concept or belief we have gained through our environmental influences.

Memories only exist to serve us. They are a summary of thought patterns that we use to quote or alter in our creating as we go. They are there to help us remember lyrics to a song, a line from a book, bodily movements, how to drive the car, recall directions to our home, and whether or not it's a good idea to place our hand on the heating element.

Once a memory is uploaded, our mind does not distinguish between reality, and the fictitious. Multiple studies in neuroscience have shown how simple it is to implant a 'false memory' into the mind of another. The same brain regions light up whether we are actually witnessing something, visualizing it in our mind's eye, feeling it or hearing it. We believe it even if we see it or not and this is how our memory can be led astray.

We can sometimes borrow other people's memories, and without knowing, believe them to be our own. This also applies to other environmental factors including what we watch in a movie, hear through audio or see when we are out and about with people around us, strangers we walk beside or see on our outings.

When we recall memories, through the processing system of our mind, memories are updated with information we carry at the time of retrieval and we adjust them a little bit each time. Our brains only remember the summary of the experience, and every time we remember something we change the memory we are accessing. We fill the gaps in our memories, so it plays out like a movie, with what we think we experienced, at the level of our conditioned beliefs upon retrieval, and not necessarily what we actually experienced. We can even create a story of what happened after the experience. Even detailed memories with vivid images, with complete belief can be completely fictitious, because our memory is so malleable. An example of the malleable memory is two or more people who shared the same event, yet recall it in many different ways.

Our brains prefer to quickly consult our past experiences rather than slowly ponder about whether or not we should do something. Do not allow your memory to lead you astray. Emotions tied to a memory leave lasting impressions and this causes all sorts of fictitious beliefs to adhere to any experience. If you experienced an embarrassing situation as a child or you got in trouble for something for example; you were playing cricket at school where you tripped or broke the bat, your memory will blow the emotion out of proportion. A memory tied with emotion is magnified, and it embeds as a long-term memory and as one of the most shameful or scary days ever. These emotionally magnified memories hang out in the background, and interrupt you from doing things in your future such as the school example, you may never wish to play cricket again. It is a type of memory that will cause you to associate "cricket with pain and humiliation" Realise this... Even these unpleasant emotionally magnified memories have fabricated gaps and we believe these or other memories are what molds us to become who we are. We give them power to dictate our experiences all the while not realizing some parts to be only fiction; and because of our ever increasing and changing conditioned thoughts, beliefs, and experiences the fiction grows as we recall these memories year after year.

Whatever was, and whatever exist right now does not have to connect. It is only your acceptance of what was that allows it to affect you now. Your brain stores imagined experiences and accepts them as real ones, you can form new memories anytime. Change the script, and be the actor who has to relearn the new lines.

Through simple awareness of our memory's unreliability we can enhance our recalls. Often we cannot distinguish a fictitious memory once it has been planted into the mind, however, we can choose which ones we want to keep as an illusion and expand upon them to serve our outcomes. We can even reject a memory particularly now that we know that it may be complete fiction. A memory is imagination. You can discipline your imagination any way you choose. Remember it is your magic pen and paper. You are the Creator of your story, past, present and future.

"Without the flexibility that comes with our memories we would also be unable to learn and would always be stuck with old memories. Instead, we are able to rewrite information when better information comes along. We can update our memory banks regularly. We can learn from our mistakes." - *Dr. Julia Shaw, author of "The Memory Illusion*

Part IV
FESTIVAL BLUEPRINT

Imagination feeds Imagination

As children we have the most vivid, uninhibited dreams, and at this time we truly were the artists of our life. We invented, laughed deep and some of us even liked to play in dirt, carefree. There are those special few enlightened beings who as they grew to an adult, continued to work on their masterpiece, they chose to follow their own advice rather than the crowd and found their way off of the evasive clone carousel. They became the influencers of society and are the creators of what we do or use now, such as;

The Wright brothers believed they could fly and they did, they created a plane. Author *Jules Verne* created stories, one with a submarine called *Twenty Thousand Leagues Under the Sea*, long before we traveled underwater. In his book *Around the World in Eighty Days.* Jules mapped out the possibility of seeing many attractions in a short period of time and today we have vacation tours that incorporate many destinations. In *Journey to the Center of the Earth*, he introduced the concept of prehistoric creatures and undiscovered flora still alive within the surface of our planet. This has triggered scientists and archeologists into thinking of the possibilities. Jules Verne left behind a lasting legacy and this infinite legacy has influenced movie makers to create film versions of his books along with inspiring the imagination of readers, viewers and inventors to think, (wouldn't it be great if it was true).

Imagination feeds imagination...

Artist, mathematician and architect, Leonardo da Vinci sketched plans of underwater crafts well before the book, *Twenty Thousand Leagues Under the Sea*. This fuelled the imagination of Jules Verne which further fuelled advances in technology and human occupied submersible vehicles were created. These submersibles fuelled the imagination of author, Tom Clancy, and this led to the invention of his novel, *The Hunt For Red October*. This novel and others fuelled the imagination of screenwriters and directors bringing to us more movies, Tom Clancy's novel, for example; gave opportunities for actors such as Sean Connery to play in the world of inventions. And the imagination continued to be fuelled giving scientists the opportunity to explore the seafloor with remotely operated vehicles.

How do we allow our imagination to flow?

Let me tell you about a great movie. In this movie a writer is inspired by watching a group of children at play. These children, brothers, are role playing in a park, one boy is laying beneath the park bench the writer sat on. This child gave the writer a fictitious reason for why he lay beneath the park bench, saying, "his older brothers put him there, his crime being that he is the youngest"

The story focuses on a writer who builds a strong friendship with this family and through observing the imaginative antics of the brothers, the writer joins in on the role playing, embracing his own child within. These antics give the writer ideas which he incorporates into a stage play. A play, that prior to its release received a skeptical response. The writer was told it would hold no appeal for upper-class theatergoers and that it was an immature concept; even the actors were dubious about playing the parts.

The circle of people in this writers' life were judgmental with what he was writing, how he was conducting himself and were concerned about what other people would think. Society has certain rules on how one is expected to act, what was considered proper and what was not acceptable; his wife even divorces him. Despite the criticism the writer continues to act and create as he felt was right within himself.

Opening night arrives and the theatre is full. The play delights the audience and proves to be a huge success and the judgmental beliefs held by the skeptics is shattered!

This movie is *Finding Neverland* where Johnny Depp portrays the writer J. M. Barrie, a man who stepped beyond the boundaries of his conditioned beliefs, he rekindled his unconditional thoughts, embraced his choice and enjoyed his childlike qualities. And it is this man, J. M. Barrie who was inspired by watching children play, embraced his imagination and this led to an invention, leaving a legacy; a story about boys who do not want to grow up, this story is *Peter Pan*. Imagination fuels imagination; From children playing, to J.M. Barrie's play, to story books, many movies, novel adaptions and spin offs such as Tinkerbell picture books and movies.

The great news is that imagination is already inherent within you. A reminder of your unconditional, unlimited imagination simply needed to be brought to your awareness. Play with your imagination, stir your giant within by finding inspiration; your journey will sprout and cultivate, and imagination will fuel imagination. Everyone has a story; it could be hibernating within your mind ready to awaken; or in your environment staring at you, waiting patiently, for you to notice. Wherever the inspiration is found for your story, it matters not, the only important thing is this is the story of your new future and will begin the moment you write upon the Universal canvas with your thoughts.

"Great things are only possible with outrageous requests." *-Thea Alexander*

The unilateral covenant

Through the media, advertising and gurus, we are told of many secrets; for good health, wealth and happiness. Secrets that when applied by the listener, does not deliver everlasting peace and happiness; and secrets that brings many dollars to those who promote such declarations. Why is it that a vast array of information exists; overloads of contradictory secrets and formulas; and why do some scams continue to be successful?

Because, there is something within collective thought that pines for more; <u>ambition</u> *(ambitionem*, "a striving for favour, courting, flattery; a desire for honour, thirst for popularity") <u>and selfishness</u> (self-seeking, self-ended and self-ful).

We dress ourselves in ways that either honour ourselves or others. We eat and think in terms of health or appropriate weight. Financial situations are portrayed as look what I have or haven't got, we want more; more money, more love, happiness, peace, better health or recognition, yet, though some of this may appear to be vain, ambition and selfishness is our natural state, without this we could never expand our infinite and unique self.

Ambition and selfishness are installed possessions belonging to the soul. We are on automatic. We cannot help but want more because we have inherited these traits well before we were born into this physical existence. We exist in an ever evolving, ever expanding and infinite Universe that requires more for expansion, we must want more, because expansion is a stream and we, the soul self, continually flow in this stream.

Ambition and selfishness is the way of a young child and baby. A baby will scream and cry; wanting to feed or to be held; pandered to, attention seeking, and never does the baby consider how another feels, such as; are they tired or busy. Children fuss and fight over toys, food or whatever it is they want or do not want. If there is something they like, the concept of sharing is foreign to them. A toddler will say such things as "mine" or "no", no if they are told not to touch something, yet, they continue to 'push the boundaries' until 'stop' is repeated over and over again, or they are physically removed from that something. So, where did their ambition and selfishness come from and why was it built into the blank canvas of a child?

A child enters this physical world protected. They are pre-installed with conditionings to reject any or all attempts by others to invade "their space"; the space within their thoughts, because when this space is tainted they become a product of their environment. A being with conditioned beliefs. This is a window for them to play and experience in the physical, through their limitless imagination.

We as adults have been conditioned to believe that selfishness, in particular, is not acceptable. We teach a child that this is inappropriate and bad behaviour, and we do this repeatedly, until we eradicate the behaviour or create beliefs of guilt for the child acting on this behaviour.

Though we the adults had the same conditioned beliefs passed onto us, this only placed a veil over what was already inherited. The roots of a tree cannot be removed only the surface appearance can be changed. We just as the tree, still have the roots, otherwise we would not exist; the tree would be dead without roots. The pre-installed protectors, ambition and selfishness, are a basic trait of our natural self and the veil has only suppressed it. This suppression has created resistance, and what we resist will persist, only, we now portray it in different ways, by desiring conditioned beliefs, such as dressing ourselves in ways that either honour ourselves or others, eat and think in terms of health or appropriate weight and look what I have or haven't got; All about me, my and I. We use our protectors in physical vain, and have forgotten that they were designed to reject any or all attempts by others to invade "our space"; the space within our thoughts, and we have neglected to refuse conditioned beliefs, so that we may only listen to our soul's voice; and follow the path of our unique desires.

Let's move onto the covenant:

Covenant: from *convenire,* "to come together, agree."

A Covenant is where parties come together to make a contract. It is agreed by promises, stipulations, and each have equal privileges and responsibilities. The covenant referred to above is bilateral. There is also another covenant known as unilateral. This is where persons are the beneficiaries and not the contributors; the beneficiary essentially has no constraint on what they decide, and the contributor, the other party accepts the decisions offered, to keep it as demanded, and to deliver the results of the decisions.

The unilateral contract is what we, the human race, have with the Divine, God. We are the beneficiaries and the Divine is the contributor. In order for this contract to pan out smoothly and benefit us for greater good, we must know, trust and believe the Divine is unlimited, all good and generous; and that any or all possibilities of experience exist. However, if we do not take responsibility of this contract; responsibility for our decisions (our held thoughts), and misuse it with lack of trust and disbelief, it carries with it harsh penalties. Penalties that stem from thoughts of lack and limitation, such as; fear, anxiety and despair. These stemmed thoughts will be contributed and delivered to us, showing up in the physical experience as abnormal results and it can be ill health, hardship or unpleasant outcomes.

Our contributor means to share with us the greater good, for each and every unique self, this must be believed and obeyed (from *obedire,* do one's duty, serve, pay attention to, give ear"). It is our duty to decide on and think only in the greater good for our unique self. To be ambitious and selfish for our own unique desires. The desires that makes our individual self truly happy.

"God made a covenant (a conditional covenant, the Divine Universal Laws) with man (humankind). 'Good' was promised to them and their children for generations if they obeyed Him and His laws; but He always warned of despair, punishment, and dispersion if they were to disobey." *(Hebrews, KGV)*

How do we obey the Covenant?

We are the stewards (from s*tiward,* "house guardian, hall, pen, guard.") of the Divine, God. And God is the God power always present within us, that which we are; the master. We, the human, as the stewards or the servants of the master, must obey by being faithful and place trust in our master, our inner God; and constantly, as well as continuingly keep this faith. We must trust in our chosen thoughts, even if we don't know where or how something can be achieved into the physical, just know with unwavering belief that our source is unlimited, and Divine only operates by providing all opportunities.

The steward fundamentally lives the same lifestyle as the master. If the steward is unfaithful and causes the estate (the mind) to suffer, by believing in lack and limitation, the servant will suffer as a result, however, through faith, rewarding beliefs and practice of trust, the dominion of the mind will prosper and the steward reaps the benefits because it shows up in the physical experience. "All power is given unto me to bring my heaven upon my earth." *(Matthew 28:18)*

Our physical self; the steward has a relationship with the master, our inner God, and this is the all-important relationship that must be above all, in our lives. We must be ambitious and selfish to our unique thoughts and never allow other opinions, unwanted outcomes to invade 'our space'. Everything we experience in the physical is the result of what we placed into our estate (the mind, our master) and we must understand that our physical possessions are owned by the master, not our physical selves because the master is the contributor; the other party, who accepts the decisions offered, and delivers the results of all decisions.

When we practice our unique thoughts and bond the relationship with the master, we place ourself in a state of non-resistance and eliminate the possibility of unwanted experiences that crush our abundance, because the master will always contribute, always give to us what we want, supply is unlimited and the master wants us to have an abundant physical experience, this is why we have unconditioned and unlimited opportunities.

As the steward we have both opportunities from, and responsibility to our master. Be faithful, trust and believe in the power of your master; The Divine, the mind, the God within, and always focus on your relationship with the master.

Do you live and act as a steward to the Divine? Do you live by the rules of your master and know your master is all powerful?

"If two of you agree on earth concerning anything that they will ask, it will be done." *(Matthew 18:19)*

This simplicity and directness of Divine Law shows us that when we ask, <u>believe</u>, we receive; God (the mind, the imagination) is the Giver, man (the steward) is the receiver!

'Top Secret' Unmasked

Many seek the deep, dark secret which has been hidden from the masses; one which when known, will reveal the path to vast opportunity in life experience, the ultimate secret to all successes.

Our layers of conditioned beliefs blended with our natural inheritance, ambition and selfishness has us listening to the secrets shared by gurus, advertising and media, however, this array of secrets is simply distorted information or fads and only shrouds the true meaning of ambition and selfishness, yet, there is a 'top secret' that turns out to be truth! This "top secret" is one that has been hidden in plain view but neglected by many.

In fact, there are two 'top secrets'. These are open secrets, secrets known by many and throughout centuries, but not widely practiced and this is because conditioned beliefs, hold disbelief and lack in knowing.

The first 'top secret' is...

"Your own wonderful <u>human imagination</u> IS God."

And...

"God is man, and exists in us and we in Him"

("Annotations to Berkeley" by William Blake).

The eternal bode of man is the imagination; and that is God Himself. Try to disprove it." - *Neville Goddard*

You, your physical self is the receiver and God; your imagination is the giver!

Neville Goddard in *"The Secret of Imagining"*, wrote:

You are an immortal being. You cannot die because you are all imagination. Man (human) is all imagination; and God truly is man; and He exists in us, and we in Him. And that immortal body of man is the human imagination...

When we read in the Bible: "I, even I, am He. I kill, and I make alive; I wound and I heal; and there is no god besides me." (Deuteronomy 32:39). This is not a being outside of you speaking; this is the Being that you really are, speaking within you, trying to persuade Himself of His own wonderful power to create. It can kill, and yet it can make alive. It can resurrect from the dead. And that is your own wonderful human imagination.

God is my pure imagining in myself. He underlies all my faculties, including perception, but He streams into the surface mind least disguised in the form of productive fancy.

Look into the world and name one thing that wasn't first imagined. You name one thing that does not now exist in your imagination – just name it. Name anything in the world that does not now exist in your imagination."

"All things exist in the human imagination (from "Jerusalem" by William Blake)"

Know, believe, trust and have faith in God, your imagination for you are the steward, the servant of the imagination and the Imagination is your 'workshop', the estate from which all will be created into existence.

Florence Scovell Shinn in *"The Power of the Spoken Word"*, wrote:

"The Truth student knows he must prove the Principle in his everyday affairs. "Acknowledge me in all your ways and I will direct your paths." "Verily, verily, I say unto you, he that believeth on me, the works that I do, he shall do also, and greater works than these, shall he do, because I go unto my Father." The man made in God's

likeness and image, (imagination). "And whatsoever ye shall ask in my name, that will I do, that the Father may be glorified in the Son." If ye shall ask anything in my name I will do it. He explained to the people that they were under a system of gifts. God was the Giver, man the receiver. The words that I speak unto you I speak not of myself but the Father that dwelleth in me He doeth the works." He told people to "seek the kingdom," the realm of perfect ideas, where all things would be added unto them. He woke them up!

Jesus Christ taught man to harness and direct thought. He knew that fear was as dangerous as uncontrolled electrical forces. Words and thoughts must be handled with wisdom and understanding. The imagination is man's workshop, and an imagination running wild and building up fear pictures, is just about as safe as riding a bucking broncho."

The second 'top secret'…

Is well known but not widely practiced and this is because conditioned beliefs hold fears of lack and limitation.

<u>You can never out give God</u>!

Do you act as your master; the contributor, who graciously gives to you everything?

Your master; God, your imagination, is generous and gives to you everything you ask for. Our master is our teacher and faith in the teacher is to do as the teacher does. We must give generously. Remember our physical possessions are not our own, we were given these by our master, therefore, when we give, we share that which belongs to the Divine. We must give willingly and often, the more we give the more opportunity we receive for a return; like attracts like, the Law of Attraction, give and you will be given. Never do this sparingly, have faith and trust that as much as you give you shall receive. It cannot be any other way; it is Universal Law. "He who sows sparingly, reaps sparingly" *(2 Cor.9:6)*.

In order to receive you must give first. Our receiving's or results will always correspond to the amount we give. If we give sparingly, we think through lack and limitation therefore we will receive sparingly including outcomes of lack and limitation. Our imagination is limitless, unconditional and unconditioned. Without this knowledge, faith and trust we operate as paupers with financial hardship, ill health, low emotions or poor relationships. All of the riches that exist now, before and to come are there for the testing and using this is the very heart of the "top secret". We are stewards of the True and Living

God; our non-physical self, our God within, the imagination. Our God within already granted us access and expects us to test, play with and share the resources.

How can you gain in the physical, and be blessed with promises of your soul's desires?

Action the 'top secret'…

The answer is just a simple word, a common, overused word that when truly understood goes deeper than the regular meaning; FAITH! from *fidem,* trust. Have faith in the power of your imagination.

When holding thoughts within your imagination occasionally refrain from asking with definite direction, this means you already assume that you; your conditioned mind, knows of a better way or process for desires and this can limit potentials that could be ideal for your unique soul's desire. Trust the wisdom and brilliance of your greater source. If you choose to be specific in your orders, finish it off with 'this or something better' and trust that your inner God knows what is truly required for your unique and everlasting happiness.

Here is another except from Florence Scovell Shinn's book, *"The Power of the Spoken Word"*:

"God's gift to man is power; power and dominion over all created things; his mind, his body, and affairs. All unhappiness comes from lack of power. Man imagines himself weak and the victim of circumstances, claiming that "Conditions over which he had no control" caused his defeat. Man by himself, is indeed, a victim of circumstances; but linked with God-power all things are possible.

Through a knowledge of metaphysics, we are discovering how this can be done. By your word you contact this power. Then, miraculously, every burden is lifted and every battle is won. Life and death are in the power of the tongue. Watch your words with all diligence. You are continually reaping the fruits of your words. And he that overcometh and keepeth my works to the end, to him will I give power and dominion over the nations."

There are no hard times in the kingdom. You may have to keep this up for quite a while, like the song of the katydids — "Katy did—Katy didn't." and so on. Finally you win out, for the truth must prevail and you have put to flight the army of the aliens. Then, when you are off your guard, the army of the aliens begins again; "You're not appreciated, you'll never be a success." You answer immediately: "God appreciates me, therefore man appreciates me. Nothing can interfere with my divinely designed success." Finally the army of the aliens is dissolved and dissipated, because you do not give it your attention. You have starved the aliens out. Starve out the fear thoughts by not giving them your attention and acting your faith. The lion draws his fierceness from your fear, his roar is in the tremors of your heart. Stand still like Daniel, and you too shall hear the rush of angels sent to take your part."

Believe and trust in who and what you are, you are imagination and imagination has always been your opportunity and responsibility. Everything up to now was first thought of in your own imagination and you the physical steward received your master's generous giving's; and you received everything you held in the imagination; everything you ask for, good or bad.

Also know that 'now' is the only point that can be referred to as existence. Before and tomorrow are irrelevant for creating. Thinking of the past or future can add resistance when we yearn for what was, or worry about a tomorrow that has not yet come. The future we desire will only come if we choose to hold new thoughts in the imagination of our 'now'. Thoughts of the past will only bring to fruition the same results, even perhaps unwanted results, if we think about past hardships.

Give wholeheartedly and often. Giving comprises of much more than money or physical items, though these are included, giving also comprises of sharing with others; your time, assistance and talent. Remember this, everything is energy; money, physical items and actions; and energy flows best when it is circulating.

"The Eternal body of Man is The Imagination, that is, God himself."- *William Blake*

"The concept of imagination is perhaps the most important key to the understanding of the opus." - *Jung*

"He who finds me finds life.
He who misses me injures himself;
All who hate me love death."
(Proverbs 8:29-31, 35, 36)

Lost!
But now I'm found

Self-discovery is an exploration in viewing our beliefs where we decide whether these ideas gained through others truly make sense to us or serve us. We must be willing to embrace new thoughts, experiences and question our practiced conditioned thoughts and beliefs. Living your unique life choices that make you feel good is to reach self-actualization- Existing as your unique energy signature.

In an age with so many distractions vying for our attention, simply by reminiscing our childhood ways will raise our imagination and begin the momentum in setting ourselves apart from the evasive clone carousel. It's a way to freedom, and unlocks the potential we were born with: unconditional, unlimited thought. We cannot reopen our unconditional minds until we let go of what is holding it, such as, adages or conditioned beliefs. Adages are sayings that become widely accepted as truth over time such as, 'life wasn't meant to be easy'. And adages have become the automatic negative thought patterns or the negative self talk we hold in our thoughts; our bully patterns that boost weakness and uncertainty. Here are some more examples; It's too hard, all the good men/women are taken, I'm so stupid, I can't do that, it won't work, I don't know how, I don't deserve, blah, blah and blah. Ridiculous thoughts that interfere with our path to abundance.

Florence Scovell Shinn in *"The Power of the Spoken Word,"* wrote;

"These negative thoughts have always defeated the manifestation of your heart's desire. They are the thought forms which you have built up in your subconscious by constantly thinking the same thoughts. You have built up a fixed idea that "Life is hard and filled with disappointments." You will meet these thoughts as concrete experiences in life, for "Out of the imaginations of the heart come the issues of life."

Let's paint a visual and develop a new tool for eradicating automatic negative thought and conditioned patterns:

In the book *Gulliver's Travels* by *Jonathan Swift*. Gulliver a captain of several ships (this is you a captain of your ship, your mind, with several possibilities), travels to remote Nations of the World (your unlimited, unconditional imagination).

Gulliver, on his journey, strikes hardship and becomes shipwrecked. He is washed ashore on an island where the inhabitants are a race of tiny people and these tiny people take this giant as a prisoner by binding him with a collection of little ropes.

Imagine that you are laying on the ground, bound down by a grid of little ropes, just as Gulliver. Each rope represents a conditioned thought, belief and automatic negative ridiculous pattern. Some of these little ropes feel tight, you can feel the discomfort as they press against parts of your body. They are only tight because other ropes are creating pressure. If you can just release a few, the discomfort will start to ease. Now, think of some patterns or beliefs you hold. Each time one comes to mind it is one of these tiny ropes.

The tiny people around you may have done well in trapping you, however, they neglected to see that in your hand you hold scissors. Scissors with the power to cut through these ropes and you begin with the easiest one you can reach, cutting it without effort. You do another, then another and each one that releases rewards you with ease from the discomfort you felt earlier. You now have more freedom to move and as you continue to cut more of the little ropes, it gets easier.

Another helpful practice in eliminating automatic negative thought and conditioned patterns is as follows:

Begin by noticing some of your negative thought patterns. Next, just observe your thoughts, do not react or respond; let them simply 'be'. For example; you are on the phone to someone who is nagging and you remove the phone from your ear. You are aware they are still on the phone, however, you cannot hear the nagging words because you stopped listening.

Allowing something to simply 'be' is acknowledgement. When we acknowledge our thought patterns we become more mindful to the thought chatter and this instantly minimizes the effect of the momentary low frequency sensation. This also allows the negative chatter to exist and removes resistance. Remember, whatever we resist will persist, therefore, it is good practice to accept even the negative sensations, after all, negative frequencies are also part of creation, the ALL and nothing is good nor bad, only our beliefs make them so.

Once you have acknowledged your minds thought

pattern place the palm of your left hand over your solar plexus (midway between bellybutton and chest). Feel the warmth of your palm and thank the negative thoughts for presenting themselves. These thoughts give you the opportunity to notice your conditioned habits. When you have completed the gratitude statement, replace the moment with a thought that feels better and follow this with an action that feels good such as; dance, hum, walk about, gardening, something that needs to get done; or whatever inspires you and brings you enjoyment.

Always use you left hand, this will subside the impact of negative emotion and the left hand is connected to the right side of the brain, the intuitive, thoughtful, and subjective part of mind. The subjective mind accepts influence of feelings and opinions; this is why you replace the negative thought with a better feeling thought. The left-brain is the logical, analytical, and objective mind. It is impartial, detached and neutral to new chosen thoughts, therefore, is not influenced to act on the change of frequency. Do this often and anytime you feel negative clutter, take back control of your thoughts and outcomes; through this practice you will notice your emotional and mental state will grow and promote your preferred 'feel good' thoughts.

We are born to evolve, to unfold, open out and expand to the success we desire, however and whatever we deem to be right; and all this with ease. Not to be bound down, held back or overpowered by the ropes of our conditioned beliefs. Our gift of choice allows us to harness new ideas and opportunities to suit ourselves.

It is this same choice we can employ to rekindle our beliefs from childhood. Our core beliefs. The ones we believed and enjoyed that ceased through conditioning and were deemed not worthy to continue. Well, the fact is, they are worthy, and satisfying for the individual who had the belief. It is these core beliefs that bring life to great ideas and freedom to be our unique self because we played in our imagination, leaving no room for expectations, we were too busy filling the spaces in our mind with happy possibilities.

As we grow to become an adult we experience change in physical growth and expansion of our senses. Our mind is overlapped with more data, notions and traditions that are shared to us from our families, television, radio, schools and any other contacts in our life that influence how we think as we age.

What of our unconditional mind? The thoughts we had from the age of one and up to our launch into adulthood.

We forgave easily, we found humor in the simplest things and we saw opportunities in the things around us.

Take some time to observe a child, be it yours, a family member, a friends or from reality TV. Take note of how natural it is for them to use their imagination through play acting, storytelling and the simplicity in how they see the beauty or fear in everyday things. We can learn or relearn a lot from children. Our asset lays in our choice to learn, to be open minded and to develop or rekindle abilities as time grows without foregoing our inner child.

Learn to recognize your pattern of beliefs and thought. The patterns can be; the way you speak, the ideas you have, the choices you make and are they really your choices? If not, where did the ideas come from, who started it, was it your parents or from a person in past generations who lived in a time very different to ours now. Or…perhaps they are memories created from a movie or through hearing another's story that has become a memory of your own!

Do these beliefs still apply today or to YOU? Maybe some of them do because the legacy in the ideas are timeless and therefore can apply to our ever evolving world. Or perhaps not because they are now out dated, and lack or limitation makes no sense, for example; Clothing stores did not exist centuries ago, nor did the vast array of choice we have for clothing to keep us warm and we have more resources including gas or electrical heating to ensure we don't freeze. We also have the convenience of home printing. Prior to these inventions people had only a printing house or service to create copies of written work and this was not affordable to all. To some, Shakespeare's first books cost the equivalent to a years' worth of bread. We are now surrounded by abundance; things, services, opportunities and there is no lack or limitation because we have many ways to attain what we desire along with a variety of choices and price scale.

Perhaps there are beliefs that don't make you feel good such as yearly events, for example: 25th December, Christmas day. You may be concerned about finances and the purchase of presents just adds stress. Or you have to attend a lunch where there is someone who makes you feel uncomfortable. What is the day of Christmas when they are many customs that celebrate it in July and other months? I shrug my shoulders, because when asking others about their customs each believe their date to be true. What of Father's Day and Mother's Day? There are many across the globe that feel sad at this time because a parent has passed away or they have not known one or both; or a parent is at work again and no quality time can be shared. These appointed days after all were created in the imagination, why must one believe that one day is more important than another, and feel bad?

What about beliefs that have changed greatly over time such as; today we respect, adore or worship actors/actresses and some see them as idols or heroes. Up until the 1800's an actress had the equivalent social standing as a high paid prostitute, also known as courtesan at the time and as 'bad ton,' one that has crawled from beneath a slimy rock located in the outskirts of Society. Even earlier than this they were considered to be no better than gypsies, this was quite an insult because gypsies, who were also travelers, were considered to be the lowest of the low. Interesting that now we have motorhomes or caravans and view this as an opportunity for travel. The word actor is from Latin *actor,* "an agent or doer, a doer, maker." Hmm, even centuries ago they were using words in the wrong context. Lucky for us that within someone's imagination they invented a better use for the word actor so that we may enjoy a host of theatre and film.

Another example is knitting. During the 1400's knitting guilds were exclusively male and guilds were established to protect trade secrets. When the industrial revolution came knitting machines were created and a few generations later knitting transformed from male dominated industry, into a sweet, staid parlour craft for Victorian women. From there it evolved to become known as old lady or grandma craft. Hmm

These examples are microscopic in comparison to the amount of changes that have occurred from the days of our ancestors and are indications that as our world evolves so should our ideas.

What are some of your beliefs? Is some of what you believe in an adage? For example: It is better to be safe than sorry, better the devil you know, the rich get richer, or you'll catch your death of cold. Let's explore this:

Who invented these and why? Why does this apply to me? Why is it better to be safe than sorry? To stay safe means, I stay in the same position with the same experiences, right! I never move, never change my circumstances or never have a go. Never give myself the opportunity for advancement, for greatness, to achieve my goal or experience more! What happened to the people that stepped out of their safe zone and ignored this adage, such as the Wright Brothers, Jules Verne or successful people who are alive today? They moved forward toward making their dream a reality and lived to experience it. That's what!

Start your own exploration. Think of some of your adages and ask yourself if you would have reached this idea had you been the decision maker at that moment in time. It is your choice, it always has been, a gift we all inherited, the power to choose.

"The art of being wise is knowing what to overlook." —*William James*

Remember, memories only exist to serve us. They are a summary of thought patterns to guide us in making a choice for the future and we should not believe everything we remember. If there is resistance or you don't feel good, you can disregard this memory, this belief and fill in the gap with a better outcome. Memories only really become a problem if they lead you toward negative personal decisions.

When you are recalling a memory avoid asking yourself closed or leading questions, such as 'what was I wearing?' or 'I was wearing a blue shirt, wasn't I?' Research shows that memories in response to unprompted recall are much more accurate than those in response to a series of questions. So if you really want to get to the bottom of something to decipher your memory, don't ask yourself too many questions!

Go to a peaceful place, your favorite area or somewhere you feel can enable a memory from childhood, such as a garden, a park, the beach or a bath full of bubble bath. Quiet your mind and allow yourself to reminisce. Picture yourself writing the story of a memory. You are writing about something that did not go well or feel good. Now, scribble over it, cross it out, tear off that bit, burn that paper, do whatever makes you see it as something you do not want, then overwrite it with what you would like to remember. Remember some of the things you thought when you were a child. You may even find some ideas, memories of play, a favorite toy or something you liked to collect that has been tucked away for years in your sub-conscious mind. Release the obstacles in the path of your imagination, enjoy recalling the things you got up to as a child. Keep building on your unconditional memories and they will manifest more, moving you toward your positive growth.

Take action, do this a few times, even the smallest step. Aim for daily reminiscing and rewriting to keep the momentum rolling. Say to yourself 'I CAN' and reawaken the GIANT within, your unconditional, unlimited thoughts, welcome the return of the festival in your imagination and your supply for stories will flow without effort.

I did this, I enjoyed remembering my childhood ways. I recalled things I liked from back then, what I wanted to be and what I believed. I wrote notes and compared my thoughts to then and now. In my 'now' note I wrote a statement; I can keep believing that being a mother, working, maintaining a home and simply surviving is my purpose in life, but the truth is I feel like there is something more, I was meant to be more than a hard working single mother, living week to week, scraping by to pay my expenses, writing shopping lists, buying the cheapest things I could find and doing daily routines.

When I was a child I wanted to be a ballerina, a TV star, to go on adventures and travel the world. As a child I would play act with whatever I found in the yard. I wasn't afraid of climbing a tree, I made mud pies, I collected caterpillars and looked after them as pets. I filled my days with things that brought me joy without focusing on the fact they brought me joy- just because. Now as an adult, I was very happy and grateful for my home, my family, my car and my work, however there was a void.

It was not until I relived my childhood memories, reviving my unconditional, unconditioned thoughts and beliefs by reminiscing, that I realized something was still missing: Me, the child bounding with unconditioned thoughts; the inventor, the tom-boy tree climber, the TV star playing pretend in the back yard having fun with my imagination, the time passing, I had no concerns, I was not afraid, I believed I could be more and have more. I laughed, danced, sang and explored. I was content and happy. That was 'me' and that 'me' never left, I just pushed it under my layers of conditioned beliefs and my unconditional ways lay waiting for me to notice.

In realizing what was missing I elevated my awareness in what should not have been present. The way my life had turned out! I was happy I had my daughter and she was fantastic, but I was not content and completely happy with all aspects in my life. I had not traveled the world, I wasn't a ballerina and I didn't climb trees anymore because adults don't climb trees, that's immature.

When I was a child I could not recall thinking when I grow up I'm going to struggle, do any job to make ends meet, raise a child on my own or live a boring, routine life. I don't think any child thinks when I grow up I'm going to be unemployed, get divorced, just work anywhere or settle for whatever is mediocre. No! A child believes they are invincible, they are capable, they can achieve it, and they can climb up that 30 metre tree, easy! I loved high jump at school and believed I could beat any height the pole was raised to. I enjoyed seeing the pole go higher and mastering that next jump. As children we truly had uninhibited and unconditional thought.

The more I reminisced, the more I remembered- regardless of the memory being fact or fiction- these unconditional thoughts began to unfold and this unlocked the festival in my imagination. I now have a consistent flow of ideas and followed by a writing process I have enabled my ability to see an idea come to fruition uninterested of how or what others think, or believe to be normal practice. I now know I have my own ideas and it is okay to show them, and it is okay to have my head in the clouds. I evolved not to an adult, but, to who I am. Did I change? I suppose it can be perceived as change, but in truth only the individual person knows who they truly are. I don't believe it's change, I prefer to think of it as 'consciously reviving'. My awakening from a hypnotic coma.

It is when we consciously revive that we are in position to take control of our conditioned thoughts, beliefs and memories. We can remove obstacles that cloud us, concern us, or dictate our path and overlook the layers of other people's ideas. We can sort through beliefs, index them into files, choose the files we want in plain view, and archive the unwanted notions into the abyss of our mind. It is also our choice to elect a time frame; by establishing which conditioned thoughts and beliefs are to hibernate permanently, or which are to lay temporarily dormant and at the given time, have permission to return to our conscious mind.

In taking control of our conditionings and rewriting our memories we can steer our own ship to float on the sparkling water of our passion, our high emotion that ignites us, excites us, touches us, warms our inner being and compels our enthusiasm. Change the phrase "I believe" to "my belief," this is a rise in your vibration attractor field, your frequency transmission. Let us not stop, never again allow interference that blocks our way to abundance, from no one, not even ourselves including diminishing intent, the intruder that dwindles our enthusiasm and hibernates our passions. We can collaborate with our inner heroes- our navigational instincts; mental faculties and beacons- these are our alerts as well as the stimulus, instinct and the urge that encourages us to keep on acting, to continue moving in the directions of our unique desires. We can question and challenge any interference. Our intuition needs no reasoning. Our spiritual perception is our unique self and guides us all to our unique happiness. We are steadfast, we can nurture our passions, maintain the momentum for our ideas, and feed our desires, even with the smallest step, such as writing it down or researching possibilities, we are on the road to our desired outcomes.

"There is no map that can show you how to leap. The map for this is somewhere in our own imagination."- *Paramananda*

"The first step toward change is awareness. The second step is acceptance."- *Nathaniel Branden*

What if?

When we are young we have no points of reference other than our environment to take our ideas further, therefore, we are a sponge absorbing what we believe is the way and become the product of our influencing environment. Whilst we ingest the influencing environment, we dream, pretend, play, invent, wait patiently and accept our ideas as something we will do when we grow up.

When a mind is stretched by new ideas and beliefs, the original thoughts are overlapped, this is crowding and reducing the powerful high emotion a child has for their ideas, and 'diminishing intent' is given the power. However, this can be altered, and it is choice, not circumstances that determines the success.

A child is not recognised as the decision maker, they are immature and viewed as young ones needing direction, therefore, we as adults influence them by showing them what would be better for them, and should they follow some golden rules such as; get good grades at school, dress neat and tidy or learn chores like cooking or yard work- then we feel they are better prepared for the outside world or the opportunities in adult life will be stronger: be it a doctor, builder, lawyer or respectable people as we believe it to be.

Should a child choose to hold on to a dream with high emotion, and <u>avert any influences</u> that can steer them away from their path until they reach adulthood by: drawing pictures, get inspired through play acting, write notes or simply continue to grow their ideas daily, they will overcome the law of 'diminishing intent'

Avert any influences! Disregard advice or overlook other people's beliefs, even those with good intention! This may seem concerning or a child can be perceived as being disrespectful. But, it will, keep them on the path to achieving their 'when I grow up' dream!

This does not mean; if a child is about to place a finger in a power socket, touch a hotplate on a stove or carry on with something that may be detrimental to themselves or others should not be stopped and the child given advice on what can occur. It refers to a child who dreams of possibilities, and these dreams do not fit within the realms of their environment, such as; they live in a remote town yet they want to be an astronaut, they want to be a dancer but their family wants them to be a builder or they want to be a literary author regardless of being illiterate.

A child informs us of their intended adult goal, whether it be verbal or by visual action. This is shown when they play; sing, dance, invent, build, tend to animals, or draw; unaware that they have passions or talents. And there are those children who extend the boundaries by delving into invention and taking apart an electrical device, or dive deep into a muddy pit to catch a worm for their experiment, and use mum's cooking pot for the container.

When a child is; taking apart an object because they need a part to make their robot, using dad's best tie to drag a box full of stuffed toys, cutting up the curtains to give their doll a new dress or soiling those new clothes to find a lost city, this is just part of their imagination. And it is this that could be perceived as a naughty child. The child is told this; that's bad or they're naughty, and they are given a reason such as; your father will be angry when he gets home. They are taught they must listen to grown-ups, the child's mind is overlapped with ideas of what is good and bad or what a child is not supposed to do, this makes them think in terms of 'getting into trouble or staying out of trouble,' and they grow to become an imitation of their atmosphere.

What if?

We learned to recognise these desires in a child, rather than; you should not have cut up the curtains, or, I paid a lot of money for those clothes. A child won't know what to do if not given a chance to explore. What if, we observed these talents, the unconditional thought, the purity in an idea, an idea that through the eyes of a child has no boundaries?

What if, we feed their desire, nurture it and maintain the idea? Yes! This can, increase our work load, we may be impatient, or at times become frustrated; the child may make a mess, we may like some of the dismantled appliances, additional costs may be incurred, the power bill has swelled and the washing has amplified. However, there is always a solution, we just need to establish it! How about: Store the best clothes in a different cupboard, have a 'uniform' for hunting dinosaurs, purchase some second hand appliances and fabric, use recycled material such as cardboard, explore the yard and find what nature has to offer, switch off the TV or computer for half an hour a day, or ask others, they may have items they would gladly give. And... take a deep breath, stop, observe the child; just to experience how much joy this brings to them. The gates of our own joy will open and give us great potential to ignite the spark in our own imagination.

Remember, when desires, inventions, hopes and dreams are acted upon and momentum is maintained it leads to succession of the goals. What if, their goal was achieved? The result could be: A fashion designer, who once used curtains to make a dress for their doll; an archeologist who always soiled their clothes as a child; or creator of the flying bus, who took apart and tinkered with electrical appliances they found around their childhood home.

And… what if it was not within the realms of your environment? Yet you:

Are bold in what you desire… Start with one simple mindset switch that will begin the process to attain your desired outcomes…Clarify your desired outcomes, write them down and practice nonresistance… Say goodbye to the old you and unwanted experiences because they are hiding the true you and your souls desire. And you…

Embraced your imagination, set up a habit, fed a desire, nurtured and maintained the idea. What if, you reawakened your unconditional, unlimited thought, your GIANT of possibilities, by reminiscing and jolting your inner child ways? What could your legacy be?

"Be not afraid of growing slowly; be afraid only of standing still". —*Chinese Proverb*

Action the brew in my head

While the following chapters are written as an example for writing literature. These examples can apply to your life experiences. All you need to do is stop for moments, and allow your imagination to take you on a journey to discover your personal adaptation and begin the creation, your life story.

So…How do I start writing?

It begins with the birth of an idea. What is your idea? Is it an opinion, your conviction, a principle, a method, a specific situation; an event significant to your experiences, a fancy or a theme.

Do you have the added ingredient, your, 'why'?

Has your imagination created your first draft floating in your mind?

Do you have a concept for a story?

Has an event triggered a notion to share it with others?

Has someone or something inspired you to scribe your thoughts?

Do you have a character you would like to immortalise, and is the urge to tell your story brewing?

Do you need to research your subject? Ideas can be developed or improved through research and promoted to growth.

What is your preferred category, perhaps comedy, romance, fantasy or adventure? Learn about the types of fiction and which one resonates for you. Remember, something that intrigues you, drives you or something you like will flow from passion.

Before you start writing, get organised. Put your wonderful ideas down on paper right away, because we potentially have roving minds and can forget the sentencing or words that appear in our creative moments. What are you comfortable with? Work out what best suits you in producing your written draft, is your preference hand written or to type. If we are conscious about the tools we use it can affect our creative flow.

When dwelling in the world of imagination we

require methods to organize our assortments. My formula for producing ideas and allowing my imagination to flow was unleashed when I grasped control over my conditioned beliefs. My ideas multiplied. I learned that a suitable plan of action was the key to ensuring my thoughts were always at hand. The information in the following chapters have become my blueprint for outlining and managing my imagination. This model for collection, plan and action continues to keep me on track and assists me in creating a wealth of ideas.

"Most 'impossible' goals can be met simply by breaking them down into bite size chunks, writing them down, believing them, and then going full speed ahead as if they were routine." —*Don Lancaster*

Collection and scraps

I keep a notebook and a pen handy. This way I can write down ideas, thoughts and observations about my experiences. I have on many occasions forgotten my notebook and when an idea appears I write it on anything I can locate at the time. I also find it helpful to draft out rough sketches in order to obtain a broader visual of my idea and when I say rough, I mean basic stick figure images. Sometimes I sketch with more detail, it all depends on my idea and how much of the visual I need to record as a reminder. I have a collection of notebooks, scrap paper, even napkins filled with words or sketches and without haste I ensure I store all my recorded thoughts in a folder for ease of access when I begin to write.

Fortunately, with today's technology, the phones we carry can be our greatest recording tool. Most have applications for voice recordings and/or a place to enter notes. This took me a little while to grasp but has now become my additional thought keeper. I still, through habit, write notes on paper and for me this is my preference. If I do record on my phone I ensure I note it in written form at my earliest convenience, this is simply my system for having all of my ideas in one file.

"Success is the sum of small efforts, repeated day in and day out." —*Robert Collier*

Sift and flow

What is on the board (is before us) cannot be ignored. When things are in plain sight we tend to focus on them and I find it much easier to have all my notes and inspirations in front of me when I zone into my world of the written word, this ensures I miss nothing.

I spread all my notes out, work over the information, and see how it all fits together. Sometimes I find some ideas that don't fit in just yet and put these aside as it will come. When anyone is absorbed in a process and ideas are focused upon, more notions will grow without effort, it always comes.

There may be occasions where I may need to trigger these waiting ideas, develop my concept or improve my subject. There IS a solution and many ways to achieve any result. I do this through research and am grateful for the abundance of resources we all have available, be it books, the internet or simply speaking with others. These are our greatest tools to kick start our inspiration when our thoughts go on a momentary, tranquil vacation.

As I sift through my collection of paperwork and place them in piles of chapters (appointed experiences to achieve) or some order that feels right, this too drives my imagination and brings forth more ideas. I write them down, regardless of how they may or may not fit in to my storyline. I find the more I sift through my notes, the better I understand my outcomes and more ideas just keep on flowing.

Our assortment of notions will always grow when we awaken the sleeping giant, our unconditional, unlimited thoughts. There will always be additional ideas, most will blend into our intended creations, yet there will be some that just need to be stored on a 'to do' pile. I have a folder I call other ideas. This is my magic box, the folder that houses a collection of my thoughts, ready and waiting to be opened for my next ventures and my method in recording the festival of potential for other stories. Stories that will come to life in my future.

Developing a birth

A movie shows us the story, but what of a book or the mind? The reader needs to visualize the authors' idea. Our imaginations have the potential to be infinite and through the written word it is expressed. In order to relay our inspiration, we need to shape and mold our ideas for our readers to understand it. **Our readers also include the Universe, the formless substance from which** everything is produced when we are using our magic pen. To enable the reader to understand my message I pretend it's a movie and someone is reading the script.

I take some of my notes even page by page, and stretch the ideas with descriptions of what I have written. For example, if it is a rabbit: what color is it, how big, are all its parts in proportion to its body, what is its name, how does it hop. If it's an emotion: how is the person standing, what is their body language, facial expression, reaction to others that may be around them, are they happy with sleeves rolled up waving their arms in excitement. If it's a scene: what color is the sky, are the plants in response to the environment frosted over from the cold or beaming erect to the glowing sun.

This is where my ideas evolve and advance to effective possibilities, the more I write and the more questions I have from my ideas, the more the body of my story unfolds. I find it very helpful to have all my notes in the chosen order in plain view again. The pile of ideas that didn't fit come to play here and I see how I can blend the mix.

Written works have a universal theme; this theme is emotion. Regardless of life circumstances readers (the Universe, the formless substance) can sense the emotions in stories be it fantasy, science fiction or mystery, through the variety of emotions shown through characters. Keep this in mind when you stretch your descriptions and be alert of the emotions that will be the outcome.

Share your ideas with people close to you, the ones that make you feel good, they may spark new ideas, and your creative flow will escalate. Research scenes, emotions or any aspects of your ideas to help you stretch it further.

It is when I visualize my vision through the eyes of readers (the Universe, the formless substance) that my urge to write propels the possibilities and my descriptions stretch for vivid understanding. It becomes a lived experience in the mind and the flow is such a natural process because of the movie playing in my imagination.

"The human mind is a channel through which things-to-be are coming into the realm of things-that-are". - *Henry Ford*

What's your fancy?

I enjoy fantasy, adventure and humor. I chose for many years to focus on fictional books aimed for children and the young at heart. This has been my guideline and I thrived on writing my preferred genre, however, as we proceed with our daily life and ingest new experiences this can change anytime we feel there is a new story to be created, I have since expanded my storehouse of preferences and enjoy an array of genre including nonfiction books now, hence I have written this book. I wanted to share my message with the intention to help others move closer to their dreams.

How to choose your genre.

We should start with what interests our individual selves, if you find a subject or genre interesting, your passion will make it interesting to others. If it bores you it will more than likely bore others, like attracts like, your written work should be something you would like to read again and again regardless of it being your written work, there's no glory when your work cannot excite you. If it excites you and makes you, that essence will come through and capture the reader (the Universe, the formless substance).

Other things to consider during your writing process is deciding what category it is, such as; romance, mystery, history, fantasy, science fiction, a biography or some combination.

Your preference to genre or classification applies in so many ways to your life experiences. By choosing your preferred outcome you will invite related experiences into your life such as, working with children, a great romantic experience, the possibility of traveling to historic sites or you become the inventor of an item that aids in evolution.

I find that research to gain knowledge, even just a small amount, will assist in moving forward to a goal. Research classifications, genres or aspects you feel you need to understand. Ask persons who will know, you may not know anyone at this stage, however, by actioning a small step and contacting someone via email or phone you will start the momentum. This momentum can only move you forward, and along with your 'why' you will continue toward the successful completion of your written work.

"The secret of getting ahead is getting started." - Mark Twain

"If you don't like how things are, change it! You're not a tree." - *Jim Rohn*

"If you don't love what you do, you won't do it with much conviction or passion."- *Mia Hamm*

"There is something in every one of you that waits and listens for the sound of the genuine in yourself. It is the only true guide you will ever have. And if you cannot hear it, you will all of your life spend your days on the ends of strings that somebody else pulls." - *Howard Thurman*

Design and plot

We should begin by asking ourselves some questions before we design and plot an outline. These can include such things as; what is my written work about, what is the storyline, the message, how do I want to feel, what is my purpose for this book in particular?

If I could describe my purpose in a paragraph what would I say? I will use this book as an example:

I wish to liberate the mind shackled with conditioned and conditional beliefs so that each may embrace the festival of their imagination through awareness of unique self and for each to discover their unlimited potential. Their unconditional thoughts.

This is my core summary and it is my 'Why'. Why I am compelled to carry this idea through to completion. My 'why' is because I believe that more inspiration only enhances our lives, surrounds us with more positive people and this legacy flows to my children, grandchildren and so on.

There are a number of reasons for a 'why.' This is determined by each individual and when ascertaining our 'why' it is essential we consciously choose a reason that is important to our individual self. We can do this by following our intuition, our instinctive feeling rather than conscious reasoning and can respond as a gut feeling to our physical senses. We can feel it in the stomach or in the heart area such as a good feeling of lightness, flutters or inner warmth. Or, it can even deliver a negative response of nausea or anxiety. It is this instinctive feeling that can help us decide our 'why.' If our intuition transmits a positive sensation, a reaction of excitement or inspiration, then this is our greatest guide to take action on our notion and claim ownership of our choices.

The decision to act on our intuition may be interrupted by our conditioned beliefs, the so called rational thinking, ideas from our environment that have obstructed our unconditional thoughts. This is because our choice represents a battle to our conditioned thoughts and beliefs; and the layered concepts will attempt to slam on the brakes or flash fear into our minds, reminding us of our boundary for thoughts; what is right, what is wrong, what others think and how we should act.

However, through reminiscing and practice we can

delve into our mind and draw from the unconditional thoughts we embodied from youth. By doing this we can recall the time we had no boundary, and choose afresh concepts we believe, that make us feel happy, and dispose of the stale layered concepts.

The key to determining your why is in choosing which side should win, your inward factors or the outward, external influences. Let your intuition guide you and identify what you will achieve from your 'why.' It could be; watching the joy in others, improving something or simply the greater good for yourself and this in turn will help your circle of people. Remember… Whatever reason you embrace to arrive at your 'why,' it is right. Right for you!

I have had many 'whys' over the years, each had a reason that was important to only me and each drove me to complete a goal, such as; 'why' did I write *Medwin's Room*, a children's novel filled with mythical creatures and other worldly dimensions. I wrote this because I wanted to share a feel good fantasy with readers, I desired to create worlds that I would dearly love to visit, even if only in my imagination.

Due to the presence of my passion pouring into this book and my 'why', readers responded with a multitude of positive feedback. This is a wonderful experience for an author. I am so happy and grateful to all those who wrote their reviews. Here is one; *"Wildly imaginative and superbly entertaining, Medwin's Room by Termina Ashton offers an uplifting journey for children and adults alike."* And this book that played in my imagination returned experiences in my physical life. I have experienced uplifting journeys, traveled to many wonderful locations, some with castles, containing characters that mimicked those in a beautiful fantasy. I am blessed with many friends, worldwide. I feel good and my world, my home environment as well as my array of opportunities is a dimension I love to experience daily.

I find that whenever I undergo a new goal it's not unusual to have multiple whys and sometimes even more whys will emerge as my ideas evolve. I welcome the possibilities of additional 'whys', these fantastic prompts fuel the fire to our passion.

Passion energises the design to our stories. I begin my design by establishing what kind of characters I am creating by building on their purpose and personalities. Here are examples:

What is there to know about the characters, what are they like, what do they want and what are they doing? Do I like them, which do I have the most empathy with? Are they misfits, rich and famous, leaders or people of action? Whose stories do I think need to be told? What are their goals? Is it rescue, love, freedom, understanding, acceptance, wealth, discovering the truth, coping with change, attaining wisdom, fulfilling a dream, coming of age, finding meaning, protector or nurturer?

The list continues and is dependent on my core idea. The core idea being my storyline and main characters.

I like to give myself a good sense of my characters. I compile notes of these descriptions, encounters or settings. I build backstories, motivations, how and why they interact the way they do. Sometimes it could be pages of my concepts, or just enough for it to make sense and fit into my core summary.

I have a separate file for characters, along with lists of words that I have seen, heard or invented to shape and personify characters. They could be a person's surname, a name of a street, the way a toddler would speak or a muddled word I have fumbled when I am tired. I use these words to either appoint a name or to create and symbolise a being.

For example: Country singer and musician Dolly

Parton, who, when meeting a young girl, simply loved the name, made up a whole story around a woman with this name and a new song was born, *"Joleen."*

In *Medwin's Room* there is a character called Pickwick. This was a word I read on a street sign and loved the sound. This word was used to build a character, a Pickwick, however, though this is the name of a single character, it is also the description of these beings in the book, such as; a dog named dog.

I also find that our daily or life encounters can help in expanding on character identities. I unroll my options by recalling who I know or have met that can be created and broadened into a character with my personal twist.

Pickwick's are mythical creatures who display a nature of kindness, love and looking after things. Though small, when they are riled they have a tall presence. Many readers have commented on these characters, they love them and say they want one- I agree, I love Pickwick! The design of this character was based on my mother. A wonderful lady, with all these traits who cared for and tended to her family. Her children are her world and should anyone wrong them her protective nature could be enraged. Her mannerism was applied for the base identity and expanded to the creation of a Pickwick.

My core idea and summary is my theme for any book. I ensure the descriptions are thorough enough for the reader (the Universe, the formless substance) to get a sense of who someone or what something is and what happens. I also aim to include my 'Why' for the reader and I keep this in mind as I write so that it is apparent as the book flows, for example; a flow of feel good fantasy so that it is suitable for any age, or chapters that trigger awareness.

An important aspect to remember is we will live with the characters and the world we create within our written works for a long time. Written works when released potentially never cease. A physical book can be disposed of, burnt or hidden; but through technology, computers (which includes the mind) store our written works, on our own personal computers to the World Wide Web and they remain in a cyber-cloud indefinitely, (just as our heads can live in a cloud, infinitely through our imagination and the formless substance stores it in the infinite Universe). So choose an idea you will not get bored with or grow to resent as the years go by. Focus your writing ideas on ones that are meaningful to you, that you will have fun working with and that you can feel proud to have written.

When plotting the outline of my written work I incorporate my loose designs in sequence. This draft allows me to manage my written thoughts in the order I would like to communicate throughout my story. It doesn't matter how descriptive or brief, it only depends on how much detail I feel I need to build on the momentum. I write an example of how I see my work beginning, what happens in the body, even break it down to some chapters. The chapters do not need to be in order immediately, nor is it necessary for all chapters to contain words at first. I find that notations of a chapter title are the greatest starting point. I use it as a guide to get simmering.

Plotting is the plan of action: this framework helps the writer to shape their story and to formulate a structure. Again, this can be done in short or long concepts. As you precede with writing your story the dynamics of your plot has the potential to grow or change direction, the draft though will be of great assistance.

Through my ideas, design and plot outline I usually conclude the ending of my written words. It is not necessarily to the precise wording, but more an ideation as to how I imagine it, is sufficient. It can be as simple as a sentence, concept or sketches. I found that having this established is like a map and helps with plotting the direction of the outcome. I know the destination, it guides me and helps me to decide on how to get there.

To sum this up as I have said in the chapter Collection and Scraps; I have found that keeping some form of note taking implement such as pen and paper or phone is essential. We are surrounded with a world of inspiration and in our moments of seeing this inspiration, by recording these notes will always have access to their reference. I find some structure or organisation to our written thoughts plays an important part when we begin our design and plot outline. Everyone has their own method for cataloguing, it doesn't matter how functional or dysfunctional it may seem to others, if it works for you, stick with it.

When my design and plot outline is ready I move onto the manuscript. This becomes my soul mate and I begin to reside in my imaginary world.

There is an essence of liberty when I begin to write. My imagination charges up my excitement and the festival playing in my imagination brings to me new adventures and experiences. Contentment and happiness of my being abound, yet, with all this activity, I feel a sense of serenity in the vacation from my physical world.

"Imagination is more important than knowledge". —

Albert Einstein

Everyone has a story inside them and on a planet that supplies billions of people, there are readers out there waiting to experience your story.

Conclusion and your awaiting future

Who were you, what do you want, who are you?

Do you tolerate a standard existence? We all have a sense there is more to us and in us. Your intimate friend, your soul sensation discontentment signals when your physical experiences do not match your unique desires. This is a reminder that your true happiness and purpose is yet to be attained and that you are capable of something more than an existence of others opinions. Allow this signal to inspire you into action so that it may grow to become a flame of possibilities and reach for your inheritance, for where you are meant to be, do and have whatever you desire.

You have choice, the ability to choose, taste, and try. You CAN become aware of your conditioned thoughts and beliefs, regardless of the distractions vying for your attention. In childhood our minds are a blank canvas, painted by the influencers of our environment and this builds the foundation of our mindset. What is your conditioned tempering? The copied patterns, ways of thinking; habits and belief in limits; the disguises that mask your unique potential. What did your environment and other generations pass onto you? What have they experienced, lived like or achieved and do you want this to be your path?

"I cannot give you the formula for success, but I can give you the formula for failure--which is: Try to please everybody." —*Herbert Bayard Swope*

Reminiscing upon our childhood and recalling some of the ways we thought when we were a child will unlock the potential we were born with and begin the momentum for our unlimited, unconditional imagination to awaken from its hibernation.

Reminisce as much as you need, find what can trigger your unconditional thought, keep the momentum rolling until you have unleashed your unlimited *wunderfoll* imagination. Remember, though that memories only exist to serve us. They are a summary of thought patterns to guide us in making a choice for the future and we should not believe everything we remember. If there are unpleasant recalls, disregard these as fabricated ones, you can choose to cut the little ropes away. The mind is not concerned with what actually occurred or not, it only waits for the story you give to it. You can place the seed of your unique desires, gain your own path, and eliminate any excuses that stand in your way, because you have…

Unconditional, unlimited thought. Imagination. It has lived with you from the day you entered this world.

Discover your stimulant. Your why! Define your 'why'. Put pen to paper, write your statement, place it somewhere you will see it often to keep firmly in your mind at moments when you might get discouraged. The 'why' provides a purpose and is a trigger to conscious revival. The why also gives certainty, such as; I have to do it, I can do it or my child needs me to do it. Certainty removes fear and pushes us to achieve that 'why'.

Write about your ideas and your desired outcomes. Writing is powerful. When we write we are also thinking, and this doubles the power of our transmission to the *"thinking stuff from where all things are made."* Formulate a process and system to suit you. Collect your ideas, sift through them and design the life of your future. Write every day, even if it's just a sentence or a few words; remember diminishing intent. Keep the momentum intact and play with your imagination daily.

Remember...

The more we practice by repetition we will discover it begins to turn into habit. This habit grows and our repertoire of inspiration begins to manifest into an endless stream of ideas, because imagination fuels imagination. It is these ideas that come to fruition and our life becomes what we have always wished for. Margaret Thatcher, former Prime Minister of the United Kingdom, borrowed, some words from an old Chinese proverb and stated this well:

"Watch your thoughts for they become words. Watch your words for they become actions. Watch your actions for they become habits. Watch your habits for they become your character. And watch your character for it becomes your destiny. What we think, we become."

Inspiration is found everywhere!

Play with your imagination, stir your giant within and the festival of ideas will flood your mind; from which your journey will sprout and cultivate.

Everyone has a story; it could be hibernating within your mind ready to awaken; or in your environment staring at you, waiting patiently, for you to notice. Wherever the inspiration is found for the story, matters not, the only important thing is this is the story of your new future and will begin the moment you write upon the Universal canvas with your thoughts.

Remind yourself…

Of the evasive clone carousel. That duplicating old patterns and beliefs is allowing others to do your thinking, to lead your way without question and to invite similar experiences over and over again. Bypass these opinions and only engage with your unique self. Go inward, recognise and connect to your accurate self. You packed mental faculties' to aide you on this trip. These are the voice of your Divine self. When you are feeling good this is your inner message, your intuition saying you have reconnected to your true self. Listen.

Guard your magic pen, your thoughts. Never let another write their thoughts into your mind and flood your canvas to the Universe, the formless substance with beliefs that do not serve you and do not make you feel good. Everything you hold to be true and write upon your mind will become a physical result, your outcome. You have let other people, other influences, write with your magic pen for many years now, it's time to take your pen back, and be in control of your outcomes. Write your own words, draw your own pictures, create your own conditioned beliefs and automatic thoughts; and keep applying your ink to your magic pad until the beliefs of the past are replaced with the ones YOU choose.

Subservient to whom? Be NOT a servant, assistant or lend support to conditioned thoughts or beliefs. You are the managing director, the boss, and the guide of your life outcomes, rather than other people's opinions that were invented through the imagination. This is the way of all and all persons have the power to reject an idea or change their circumstances in this moment, to whatever they will it to be, because it is YOU who has control over your beliefs – beliefs that create the path in life. Carry and be inspired by your unique ideas regardless of what the masses do or what is expected of you. Replace your conditioned beliefs, your patterned thinking with your own perceptions, make choices to live your existing reality in your own way and with passion so that it may be archaic *(arkhe)*, a new beginning for you; a time of merrymaking, amusement and festivity. You will have much to celebrate because you WILL achieve your soul's desires when you say goodbye to your conditioned beliefs.

Remember, there is no right or wrong. Perception of right or wrong is only created through a belief, an invention you were told to be true. Every belief, idea or conditioned belief is only an opinion. Create your own unique opinions.

You are the Co-Creator, your core IS the Divine Creator and the Genie of your own experiences. You carry with you all the abilities to create as you go, at any given moment and the free will to choose how you wish it to play out. Your wish as and when you command.

Today, is your moment in truth. To live and be your own truth, truth as you choose it to be. Yesterday is just memory, a memory that contains missing pieces and really plays no relevance in what you draw upon the Universal canvas today. Right now you can draw whatever pleases you.

Boost your vibrational frequency and bring to fruition your desired outcomes. You CAN:

Remind yourself often of who you are, you are a Creator! You are God; Pure imagination!

Acknowledge and accept what you are, you are a Supreme; it's time to love the greatness of your unique self.

Recognise your pattern, conditioned thoughts and beliefs. Face the invented fears and the hypnotic states that play only in your imagination. Laugh often, even by force to begin with as this will alter the frequency and trick you mind into thinking you are happy; then you can move to new possibilities.

Embrace your imagination, play often, write and sketch in a journal, remember that you have unlimited thought, just see where it takes you.

Observe the diversity around you, and have appreciation in all things. Good or bad it is all creation, and helpful guides that teach us what makes us feel good or not.

Write, think and speak words of gratitude for your experiences and the opportunity to play this game of life. Let your thoughts wander to all things you are grateful for, it could even be the legs you have to walk with, the eyes that help you see your legs, or the person who smiled graciously when they served you at the supermarket. This reminds us of how fortunate we are and accelerates vibrational frequency. Surprise yourself with gratitude and you will thank yourself tomorrow.

Practise listening to your navigational instincts, your mental faculties as well as your beacons, and disregard outgoings if your beacons alert you. Practice being attentive to your God within that watches over you and never sleeps; your intuition. It is your magic path, straight line and shortest route to confirmation of true self; and the yay or nay for the next step towards your unique bliss and greater good.

Give wholeheartedly and often. Give without expectation. Give your time, assistance and talent to others as well as money and physical items, after all, you, just as the apple seed are the seed of source, you can always and endlessly create greater, stronger and bigger apples, and your master: your contributor, IS unlimited; and an abundance source for more. Remember, everything is energy; money, physical items and actions; and energy flows best when it is circulating.

Surrender any need for perfection, this cannot exist because energy is always vibrating, moving and changing from moment to moment.

Inspire often, inhale and exhale. Your breath is your physical life force, place focus on it when you wish to reset the frequency or bypass the critical mind, anytime and anywhere. Choose a pleasant frequency because every moment creates the truth of the future.

Reset with physical movement to reclaim your focus and change the frequency. Walk about, jump, skip, clap your hands, dance, or simply shake your body.

Be introspective (Meditate) daily to calm the clutter in your mind and hear your soul's voice.

Surround yourself with an environment that will assist in creating your desired results, this includes the people around you. Avoid gossips, those who speak of hardship and ignore ones that speak of things you do not desire. Their words, opinions and beliefs will bring these into your outcomes. Instead, empower yourself with words and people who enjoy life. Remember less is more, better to speak less words and have one happy person in your environment than be popular with the negative ones.

Research word origins, find and practise using power words, repeat them often so that you may transmit the unique frequency of your desires. Have fun with this as well. There are many eye openers to be found along with humorous surprises such as; Avocado, from Aztec culture meaning, "testicle." (my son was researching origin words for various fruit and came across this one, hmm).

Be the non-conformist, the heretic who is 'able to choose."

Live on purpose. Purposely chose your desired outcomes.

Make a pledge to yourself to gain control of your results. Never stop, any of the above, because in every moment you are creating your outcomes, and the Universe, the formless substance, is listening, waiting to give to you everything you ask for.

Imagination is;

God

The mind

Unconditional and Unconditioned thought

Unlimited thought

An invention

A fancy

Thought in production

The GIANT within you!

A preview of life's coming attractions

Festival of the Imagination is:

"Time set aside to make visible."

There is no single answer to all the questions of life and no one has YOUR answer. We all are playing a game of life, and we the <u>Soul</u> Creators - the Supreme beings who are primarily mind and matter are the players; and we create as we go.

YOU have the ability to change today's circumstance to a happier and abundant future. Just as Einstein YOU are a GENIUS (from root *gene*- "to produce, give birth, beget"). The one simple answer is…. Choose and Make it your own. Your unique self.

What will it be, and always remember **it's your choice.**

You are **AWARE**. Now go create the life you desire.

And what if?

You achieved all your unique desires.

Imagine…

Acknowledgement

"To my unconditional, joyful son. You personify love, your presence and incredible insight adds phenomenal beauty to my life and all who have the fortune of meeting you."

"To my vibrant, joyful daughter. You gave me the magic 'Why' and your incredible presence brings a lifetime of happiness to me daily."

"To the incredible people who shared their great wisdom. Peggy McColl and Bob Proctor, I embrace you. You taught me to expand in knowing how extraordinary we all are, what we are capable of and you both do it with such clarity. Thank you"

"To Nik Halik, the wonderful forward thinking astronaut and entrepreneur with his Thrillionaire mindset, who reminded me of how enormous my inner self really was.

"To my supportive and loving friend Malanda and her family. My life is an art gallery filled with an array of beautiful people and lifelong talent to be admired."

"To all my friends, for your love, support and the valuable understanding you give when I vacation into my writing. My life is extraordinary with you in my experience."

About the Author

Termina Ashton, also known as 'The Happy Magnet', has the uncanny ability to tilt the odds so the best will happen. She resides with her family in Queensland, Australia where she lives a lifestyle of fun, joy and opportunities, and believes in navigating her own world of experiences through imagination, and Feng Shui. Termina, a mentor, author, illustrator, Feng Shui expert, and an interior designer has worked on many projects both residential and commercial including an open design radio station, Fox Studios and a variety of set designs where her own artwork was exhibited for TV and film.

Termina began writing novels to put down on paper the rampant images and adventures that filled her mind, and in doing so, has captured the imagination of children and adults all around the world. Termina is delighted her books have become so popular and is equally delighted when some describe her as Australia's answer to Enid Blyton. Termina believes a reason for the popularity is...

"No matter how old; we all like to escape into the world of imagination and creating my world is what I do, anything is possible, we should all endeavour to follow our passion, everyone has talents, push up your sleeves and take action. There is joy in doing what we love and the results are always wonderful"

Festival of the Imagination is one of many non-fiction books by Termina. Termina calls herself a student of self-actualization. It was through her studies and introspection practices that she was able to tap into her unique soul signature and states that she is guided by source. *"At all times we carry with us all the answers. There is nothing in the physical world that will truly give us the ultimate answer; our unique soul print and purpose in life; and it is because of this only ourself has the true answers for what makes us happy or why we are here. We only require external tools, or mentors to get us started and guide us in a direction towards connecting with our soul's voice. With the right tools and mentors we are on our way to unleashing our true, powerful self."*

Termina credits self-actualization practices for her success and harmony in her life. Another one she credits is

Feng Shui as a guide to alignment for choices. *"It was through my studies and practice of Feng shui that I discovered the importance this ancient art plays in our life. 33% of our experiences are created through our physical visualization board, our environment. When we apply the principles of Feng Shui our lives become the choices we desire, we are in control of our own experiences at all times and good fortune is attainable. Through Feng Shui I have seen improvements and successes in my own life along with the many others who have appointed my services."*

For more information about this author

and other books:

www.terminaashton.com

www.terminafengshui.com

www.thehappymagnet.com

www.ingramcontent.com/pod-product-compliance
Lightning Source LLC
Chambersburg PA
CBHW050654170426
43200CB00008B/1288